AWAKENINGS

DISCARD

AWAKENINGS

Thomas Keating

CROSSROAD • NEW YORK

1991

The Crossroad Publishing Company
370 Lexington Avenue, New York, NY 10017

Chapters 23–25 and 27–30 previously appeared in the author's
And the World Was Made Flesh, Copyright © 1983
by Cistercian Abbey of Spencer, Inc.

Printed in the United States of America
Typesetting output: TEXSource, Houston

Library of Congress Cataloging-in-Publication Data

Keating, Thomas
    Awakenings / Thomas Keating.
      p. cm.
    ISBN 0-8245-1044-5
    1. Catholic Church — Sermons. 2. Sermons, American. I. Title.
BX1756.K36A82 1990
252'.02 — dc20
                                    90-36054
                                      CIP

ACKNOWLEDGMENTS

Scripture texts used in this work are taken from the New American
Bible with Revised New Testament, copyright © 1986 by the Confra-
ternity of Christian Doctrine. All rights reserved.

CONTENTS

PREFACE

These random homilies are based on the premise that Christian life is a process of spiritual growth and transformation. Each new level of growth brings with it a gradual or sudden burst of understanding, a kind of awakening. The meaning of the Gospel changes as we change. This growth takes place without rejecting the knowledge that went before and manifests itself through the ever-increasing understanding of the example and teaching of Jesus.

EVENTS IN JESUS' MINISTRY

1

THE END OF OUR WORLDS

When he heard that John had been arrested, he withdrew to Galilee. He left Nazareth and went to live in Capernaum by the sea, in the region of Zebulun and Naphtali, that what had been said through Isaiah the prophet might be fulfilled:

Land of Zebulun and land of Naphtali,
the way to the sea, beyond the Jordan,
Galilee of the Gentiles,
the people who sit in darkness
have seen a great light,
on those dwelling in a land overshadowed by death
light has arisen.

From that time on Jesus began to preach and say, "Repent, for the kingdom of heaven is close at hand."

(Matt. 4:12–17)

Advent is the liturgical season that celebrates the theme of divine light. This great light, incarnated in Jesus, confronts any kind of darkness, illusion, ignorance. If you reflect for a moment on the natural cycles of life, our world is always coming to an end. The world of the womb comes to an end at birth; the world of infancy comes to an end at about age three; childhood comes to an end at adolescence; adolescence at young adulthood; young

3

adulthood at the middle-age crisis; then come old age, senility, and death. Life is a process. The experience of growing up or the decline of physical energy forces us to let go of each period of life as we pass through it. Thus physical life is always giving way to further development. It should be no surprise, therefore, that Jesus invites us to let the privatized worlds of our emotional attachments, preconceived ideas, and prepackaged values come to an end.

One of the messages of Advent, especially the theme of the end of the world, is not so much about *the* end of the world — nor even about physical death which is the end of the present world for each of us — as about all the worlds that come to an end in the natural and spiritual evolution of life. Thus, every time we move to a new level of faith, the previous world that we lived in with all its relationships comes to an end. This is what John the Baptist and later Jesus meant when they began their ministries with the word, "Repent." The message they meant to convey was, "It's the end of your world!" Naturally, we do not like to hear such news; we don't like change. We say, "Get rid of this man!"

The process of conversion begins with genuine openness to change: openness to the possibility that just as natural life evolves, so too the spiritual life evolves. Our psychological world is the result of natural growth, events over which we had no control in early childhood, and grace. Grace is the presence and action of Christ in our lives inviting us to let go of where we are now and to be open to the new values that are born every time we penetrate to a new understanding of the Gospel. Moreover, Jesus calls us to repent not just once; it is an invitation that keeps recurring. In the liturgy it recurs several times a year, especially during Advent and Lent. It may also come at other times through circumstances: disappointments, personal tragedy, or the bursting into consciousness of some compulsion or secret motive that we were not aware of. A crisis in our lives is not a reason to run away; it is the voice of Christ inviting us to accept more of the divine light. More of the divine light means more of what the divine light reveals, which is divine life. And the more divine life we receive, the more we perceive that divine life is pure love. ✗

Whenever we accept the invitation to let go of our present level of relating to Christ for a new one, it may feel scary. A comfortable relationship with Christ — our own little world of reading, prayer, devotions, or ministry — is good. But just as the life process moves on day by day, so the grace of Christ relentlessly calls us beyond our limitations and fears into new worlds. Like Abraham, the classical paradigm of faith, Jesus asks us to leave land, family, culture, peer group, religious education — everything that we might cling to in order to establish an identity or to avoid feeling lonely. All of this Christ gently but firmly calls us to leave behind saying, "Go forth from your father's house and country and come into the land that I will show you."

The call to contemplative prayer is a call into the unknown. It is not a call to nowhere, but it is nowhere that we can imagine. Each time we consent to an enhancement of faith, our world changes and all our relationships have to be adjusted to the new perspective that has been given to us. Our relationship to ourselves, to Jesus Christ, to our neighbor, to the Church — even to God himself — all change. It is the end of the world we have previously known and lived in. Sometimes the Spirit deliberately shatters those worlds. If we have depended upon them to go to God, it may feel as if we have lost God. We may have doubts about God's very existence. It is not the God of faith we are doubting, but only the God of our limited concepts or dependencies; this god never existed anyway. Pure faith is the purification of the human props in our relationship to God. As these are relinquished, we relate more directly to the divine presence, even though it may feel like the end of our spiritual life.

And so the second part of Jesus' message is important. If you repent and are willing to change, or willing to let God change you, the kingdom of God is close. In fact, you have it; it is within you and you can begin to enjoy it. The kingdom of God belongs to those who have let go of their possessive attitude toward everything including God. God is pure gift; we cannot possess him just for ourselves. We can possess him only by receiving him and sharing him with others.

2

LIVING AS IF GOD WERE ABSENT

When he disembarked and saw the vast crowd, his heart was moved with pity for them, for they were like sheep without a shepherd; and he began to teach them many things. By now it was already late and his disciples approached him and said, "This is a deserted place and it is already very late. Dismiss them so that they can go to the surrounding farms and villages and buy themselves something to eat." He said to them in reply, "Give them some food yourselves." But they said to him, "Are we to buy two hundred days' wages worth of food and give it to them to eat?" He asked them, "How many loaves do you have? Go and see." And when they had found out they said, "Five loaves and two fish." So he gave orders to have them sit down in groups on the green grass. The people took their places in rows by hundreds and by fifties. Then, taking the five loaves and the two fish and looking up to heaven, he said the blessing, broke the loaves, and gave them to [his] disciples to set before the people; he also divided the two fish among them all. They all ate and were satisfied. And they picked up twelve wicker baskets full of fragments and what was left of the fish. Those who ate [of the loaves] were five thousand men.

(Mark 6:34–44)

This occasion is one of those impossible situations that arise regularly in the course of ordinary life. It was late in a long day; a crowd of people far from home and nothing to eat. The disciples, seeing the situation, had a solution. They went to Jesus and said, "It's time to send the people away so they can find food and shelter at some crossroads." They did not see God in the situation; they saw just the human predicament. Jesus, of course, not only saw the human situation; he also saw the presence of God in it. The perspective is quite different when, like Jesus, one is sensitive to what God is trying to do.

Saint Teresa of Avila says that every difficulty in prayer comes from one fatal flaw, that of praying as if God were absent. Our spiritual journey as a whole has the same fatal flaw: seeking God as if he were absent. Everyday life has the same flaw: we live as if God were absent. One of the favorite ways of living thus, is to keep putting off our search for God, our prayer, or our conversion until after our immediate problems have been cleared up. We survive difficult situations in the vain hope that someday, somewhere, we will have the time to do spiritual reading, to get good direction, to do penance, to become a saint, or to live in a monastery. If you have made a retreat, you know that spiritual practice goes better in solitude. You may say to yourself, "Wouldn't it be great if I could live in a retreat atmosphere all the time? And since they do this in monasteries, I think I'll apply to the Trappists or the Carmelites."

This is a favorite temptation of almost everyone on the spiritual journey. We can't see the presence of God right where we are nor in the precise situations in which we find ourselves. On the contrary we think, "If only I had the ideal circumstances for prayer, everything would be fine. The thought of God would always be with me. I would pray all the time like the holy monks and cloistered sisters."

I'm not sure that monks and cloistered sisters are praying anymore than you are. They have problems too. If they live on a farm, the same temptation arises: "I'll give more time to prayer after the harvest." If they are bookkeepers, "I'll have time to pray after I pay the bills this month."

Here is the classic temptation by which we postpone living in the presence of God to some future time. Some examples of it: "I will give time to prayer when the children grow up; when my husband gets over his illness; when I no longer have to work so hard; when I can finally deal with personality problems at the office." In other words, "I'll put my mind on the spiritual journey as soon as my immediate problems are over." Our response to life is to put all our energy into surviving the difficulties of the moment believing that only when these are settled will we be able to practice the presence of God. We maintain the illusion that God is not here now; that God is not in this everyday difficulty. This human way of judging is a lack of faith. We are like Philip who said to Jesus at the Last Supper, "Lord, show us the Father and it will be enough for us."

Jesus' reply was, "Philip, have I been with you all this time and you do not know me? He who sees me has seen the Father."

If the ordinary situations of life could speak to us, they would say, "How is it that you don't recognize us? One who sees us sees God." God is present in difficulties and in impossible situations. His presence is there not only ontologically, because his being is everywhere, but also because the divine action is present in every event. Suppose on a certain day we are saying devout aspirations as we drive along the road and suddenly have a flat tire. When we can't find the jack, all our prayers go out the window. We try to thumb people down and nobody stops. Pretty soon we are totally upset. We call for a tow truck. Only when we get home and have the car in the garage, do we start to think of God again. Where was God during that situation? Did he just disintegrate?

We need to cultivate what Bernadette Roberts calls "everyday God." The X-ray eyes of faith do not wait until everything is ideal or peaceful before relating to God. Faith says, "Well, this is a strange situation, a desperate situation, an impossible situation. What is God saying to me or asking me to do?"

At the Last Judgment, according to the parable, God's servants will say, "Lord, when were you thirsty or hungry or in prison or naked." And he will reply, "Whenever you did this to the least of my little ones, you did it to me."

Impossible situations may be due to other people, disease, disaster or just immense inconvenience. How we react is our response to God's presence. Living daily life as if God were absent is the fatal flaw of the spiritual journey. The idea that God is absent is just a thought or feeling. If you can shatter that illusion and disregard the feeling, you have it made. God cannot be absent. Treating him as if he were is an insult. It is like saying to God, "You're not in my life; not, at least, in this situation. I'll pray when I get off this plane; when this lousy sermon is over; when I finally get my divorce; when this painful situation at the office is settled; when the energy that I need to survive this impossible situation is once again available."

Jesus could see in that crowd of hungry and weary people, in that impossible situation, God inviting him to work a miracle. He was moved only by what he saw the Father doing. His sensitivity to the divine compassion so heightened his perception that in a situation where there was no food he knew the Father would do something to provide it. If he had seen that situation as just one more impossibility and sent everyone home, God's concern for this human need would not have been manifested.

In daily life the Spirit is speaking in various ways. Christ is present under different disguises. In human tragedy, there is something that the Father wants us to do to bring healing. The contemplative dimension of the Gospel keeps heightening this sensitivity. When one follows the inspiration of the Spirit, results occur that could not possibly have been foreseen. Hence, the need to cultivate God's presence and action in situations that seem impossible to do anything about. The mystery of Christ is at work in everything, however humble or humdrum. Our response can be inspired by the false self or by the Spirit. If it is by the Spirit, the consequences are immense both for ourselves and for others, and perhaps for the whole human family.

3

CHRIST IN THE STORM

Then he made the disciples get into the boat and precede him to the other side, while he dismissed the crowds. After doing so, he went up on the mountain by himself to pray. When it was evening he was there alone. Meanwhile the boat, already a few miles off shore, was being tossed about by the waves, for the wind was against it. During the fourth watch of the night, he came toward them, walking on the sea. When the disciples saw him walking on the sea they were terrified. "It is a ghost," they said, and they cried out in fear. At once [Jesus] spoke to them, "Take courage, it is I; do not be afraid." Peter said to him in reply, "Lord, if it is you, command me to come to you on the water." He said, "Come." Peter got out of the boat and began to walk on the water toward Jesus. But when he saw how [strong] the wind was he became frightened; and, beginning to sink, he cried out, "Lord, save me!" Immediately Jesus stretched out his hand and caught him, and said to him, "Oh you of little faith, why did you doubt?" After they got into the boat, the wind died down. Those who were in the boat did him homage, saying, "Truly, you are the Son of God."

(Matt. 14:22–33)

Let us read this dramatic text from the perspective of our own experience of grace. On the Feast of Pentecost the Spirit of Christ, poured out on the original disciples, is poured out on us. Year by year, this feast refines our receptive apparatus so that we can tune in to the more profound, delicate, and fascinating messages of the universe and its source.

Jesus had spent the night in prayer. How was he to bring his disciples to a better understanding of the kingdom of God? The kingdom involves a change of values at the deepest level. This is a project that terrifies most people. Theoretically, it would be great to grow up. Actually, we usually say, "Let's wait a few days, weeks, years."

Jesus was inspired by the Spirit to use this opportunity to bring his disciples to a deeper level of understanding. The Gospel is not so much a teaching as a transmission. From the Old Testament we know about Elias' meeting God in the hurricane, in the earthquake, and in the fire. A hurricane shatters rocks, picks things up and throws them down, blows everything away. An earthquake unsettles the ground under you. Fire is something you run from as fast as you can. The hurricane and earthquake are symbols of opposition from outside. The fire is an image of interior temptation. The hurricane, the earthquake, and the fire are the difficulties and the trials that overtake us in the course of the spiritual journey.

The disciples in the boat, battered and beaten by the winds and the waves, are symbols of those who try to obey the Gospel and meet various kinds of opposition. They come upon the naive disciple who thinks that having accepted Christ, prayer and meditation are going to provide a magic carpet to bliss — or even better, to financial success in this world. *No chance!*

In the midst of this storm, a figure emerges out of the darkness. What the disciples thought they saw is something that one might easily visualize at 3 a.m.: "It's a ghost!" Jesus is walking on the water. He emerges out of the storm. This means that, in a real sense, he is *in* the storm, *in* the wind, *in* the waves.

Peter hears the invitation to come to Jesus over the water. In other words, Peter is invited to lay hold of Jesus in the midst of opposition, disappointment, and the stretching of faith. Peter is the symbol of those whose faith perceives that the wind is not just wind, but Christ, inviting us to find him in the midst of opposition and temptation.

The immediate response of the disciples is terror and they start crying out, fearful of the ghost that is bearing down on them. Jesus calls to them, "Look! It is really I! Don't be afraid."

Then Peter says, "Lord, tell me to come to you over the water."

Jesus says, "Come!" Peter steps out onto the waves. He is walking on the water! He reaches out for the Lord in the midst of the elements. He hangs on for dear life to the presence of Christ in the midst of the storm.

All of a sudden, the wind increases. A wave splashes against his legs and the spray moistens his face. Now there is a slight shift from his focus on Jesus to the actual situation. He begins to sink. He cries out, "Lord, save me!" Immediately, Jesus reaches out and pulls him into the boat. There comes a great calm and the apostles in astonishment proclaim, "Truly, you are the Son of God!"

It's nice to know that we are not expected to succeed the first time we try to see God in the midst of difficulties from within or from without. We miss the first few times. When we start sinking, we have only to call for help and God seems to moderate the intensity of the trial so that we can get a brief rest and try again. The "again" for the apostles was Jesus' crucifixion and they all sank. Trials always *look* like impossible situations. We try to accept them but things get too tough. Our faith and trust wither and we begin to sink. We call for help and Jesus rescues us. There is a brief calm. If we continue the journey, the wind and the waves start up again. Again we try to find Jesus in the particular difficulty; again we start to drown; he pulls us out. This is the story of everyone's spiritual journey. The only mistake is to go down and stay down; to sink and not yell for help.

Little by little we are able to hear the still small voice in the hurricane, the earthquake, or the fire. God is hidden in difficulties. If we can find him there, we will never lose him. Without difficulties, we do not know the power of God's mercy and the incredible destiny he has for each of us. We must be patient with our failures. There is always another opportunity unless we go ashore and stay there. A No-risk situation is the biggest danger there is. To encounter the winds and the waves is not a sign of defeat. It is a training in the art of living, which is the art of yielding to God's action and believing in his love no matter what happens.

4

THE CANAANITE WOMAN

Then Jesus went from that place and withdrew to the region of Tyre and Sidon. And behold, a Canaanite woman of that district came and called out, "Have pity on me, Lord, Son of David! My daughter is tormented by a demon." But he did not say a word in answer to her. His disciples came and asked him, "Send her away, for she keeps calling out after us." He said in reply, "I was sent only to the lost sheep of the house of Israel." But the woman came and did him homage, saying, "Lord, help me." He said in reply, "It is not right to take the food of the children and throw it to the dogs." She said, "Please, Lord, for even the dogs eat the scraps that fall from the table of their masters." Then Jesus said to her in reply, "O woman, great is your faith! Let it be done for you as you wish." And her daughter was healed from that hour.
(Matt. 15:21–28)

This text has great significance for the spiritual journey. In previous texts we have seen Jesus giving examples of how to sense the infinite concern of God, in daily life and in the impossible situations in which we are least inclined to look for God. We have seen Peter and his companions as symbols of our efforts to find God in the storms of life and to perceive him emerging out of the winds and the waves. We are asked to go further than that and to respond to his presence. Peter's response was to walk on the water, the symbol of maintaining peace amid the tribulations and ups and downs of daily life.

Now we come to the real stuff. How do we find God in his apparent absence, rejection, and abuse? That is something else. This episode is a description of how to respond when prayer gets difficult, when the interior life falls to pieces, or when the night of sense descends upon our spiritual nest. It descends in order to get us out of the nest. The divine eagle has come to shove us into reality. This marvelous episode tells us about the night of sense from God's point of view and about his strategy in the mysterious dryness, absence, and darkness that follow the springtime of the spiritual journey.

The Canaanite woman seems to have been a pagan. Jesus points out that sometimes those outside the household have more faith than those inside. She had probably heard that Jesus was most gracious in granting requests to cast out demons. Thinking he was an easy touch for her request, she was not expecting any trouble. Perhaps she had seen others go to Jesus with the same request and receive without difficulty what they requested. So she said, "Lord, Son of David, have pity on me. My daughter is terribly troubled by a demon."

She stood there waiting for an answer, perhaps expecting to hear some reassuring invitation such as, "Bring your daughter here," or "She is already healed." If he had decided not to heal her, he could have at least said, with a gentle pat on the shoulder, "There, there; go home and offer it up." This is the sort of thing you sometimes hear from well-meaning people when you are in trouble — to your great consternation.

The text says that Jesus did not say a word. He was just silent. Is this an answer to prayer or isn't it? I venture to say that silence is as good an answer to prayer as the granting of our request. If we accept silence as an answer, we may perceive its purpose. For example, it could mean that it is not the right time; that we are not ready for an answer; or that we are asking for the wrong thing. The primary purpose of prayer is not to change God but us, and if we are not prepared to change, there is nothing to say.

In the night of sense, we come for our interview with God and he does not show up. This is all right for a while but eventually the question arises: What is the use of coming if God never shows up? I am referring to his apparent failure to show up. He is there but he is there at a different level than we are. In the case of the Canaanite woman, the point of this silence is to bring her from the level of faith from which she starts out, to the level of faith that she manifests at the end. This strategy adjusts the divine action to our human condition. It does not represent God's choice. The only way God can bring somebody to a new level of faith is to challenge their present level. Many of the episodes in the Gospel manifest this. We have only to think of the centurion who got what he wanted instantly and the man whose son was at the point of death whose request to go down to his house Jesus refused. To the centurion he said, "I'll come right way." Why this strange shift in response from one person to the other? One has the fullness of faith and does not need to have it tested; the other's faith was not strong and needed the challenge of the divine silence.

In this dialogue the woman is raised from one level of faith to another until she attains an extraordinary level. She goes to the apostles as we might turn to the angels and saints for help. The disciples said, "Let's get rid of this woman." They were not helpful at all. Jesus did not answer their request either. But notice what he said: "My mission is only to the lost sheep of Israel." He appeals to his official mission. She is a pagan and his mission is to those of the household of Israel. On one level this is good reasoning and shows our Lord's sensitivity to do only what he sees the Father doing. He does only what he is sent to do; he does not want to exceed it. A mission or ministry always presupposes that we are prepared to function on God's terms.

The Canaanite woman interpreted this statement to mean, "Nothing doing; I only work miracles for Israelites. Sorry." In response, she comes forward and prostrates at his feet, full length, groveling in the dust. Her cry is: "Help!" This is the prayer that Meister Eckhart says pierces the heavens. It is totally focused on one objective. This cry of desperation from a person who feels rejected by God in prayer says everything — a plea, it would seem, that would touch the heart of a stone. And yet Jesus gives no reply. What has become of the divine mercy?

But the divine mercy is not sentimentality. It relentlessly puts the ultimate realities of life before her so that she can say with total honesty, "I can't do it myself; I must have your help!" And God is saying nothing.

"It is not right," Jesus says, "to take the food of the children and to throw it to dogs." How could Jesus say such a thing? The Canaanite woman is not put off by this insult any more that she was by his silence and rejection. She answers in effect, "Lord, you are right. But have you thought of this possibility? I'm not asking for the food of the children; I'm not asking for a loaf of bread. Even the dogs under the table sometimes pick up a few crumbs that fall by mistake. How about dropping me one of those crumbs?"

Jesus responds, "Oh my dear lady, your faith is terrific! You can have anything you want — the whole world, the universe, anything!" Everything belongs to those who have reached this level of faith. The cosmos was created for them.

Such is the scenario; it keeps being played out in our lives. We can accept it like the Canaanite woman or back off.

5

THE SINFUL WOMAN

Then each went to his own house, while Jesus went to the Mount of Olives. But early in the morning he arrived again in the temple area, and all the people started coming to him, and he sat down and taught them. Then the scribes and the Pharisees brought a woman who had been caught in adultery and made her stand in the middle. They said to him, "Teacher, this woman was caught in the very act of committing adultery. Now in the Law, Moses commanded us to stone such women. So what do you say?" They said this to test him, so that they could have some charge to bring against him. Jesus bent down and began to write on the ground with his finger. But when they continued asking him, he straightened up and said to them, "Let the one among you who is without sin be the first to throw a stone at her." Again he bent down and wrote on the ground. And in response, they went away one by one, beginning with the elders. So he was left alone with the woman before him. Then Jesus straightened up and said to her, "Woman, where are they? Has no one condemned you?" She replied, "No one, sir." Then Jesus said, "Neither do I condemn you. Go, [and] from now on do not sin anymore."

(John 8:1–11)

The Temple of Jerusalem was an awesome place: lots of arches, walls, towers, ornamented floors, and the great altar of sacrifice. It was there that Jesus used to teach during the day, while in the evening he retired to pray on the Mount of Olives. In the Old Testament "olives" are a symbol of the divine mercy and healing, a key to understanding this remarkable scene.

As Jesus resumes his teaching in this awesome structure, a woman is dragged in front of him. It does not take long for us to perceive that this is a trap; it did not take him long either. His enemies were becoming aggressive at this point and had figured out a clever plot to question him in such a way that he would have no way out. Whatever he said would be held against him. They would then accuse him and perhaps have him discredited.

The question was, "We have caught this woman in an obvious sin and the Law clearly states that such a woman should be stoned. What is your judgment?" If he said, "Don't stone her," he would be contradicting the Law. If he said, "Stone her," he would be contradicting the whole thrust of his teaching, which was that the author of the Law was Abba, the God of infinite compassion and concern for every living thing. This was a revolutionary idea. The God of Israel up to that time had been generally regarded as the God of armies, the God of thunder and lightning, the God of strict justice, Israel's Lawgiver. Jesus' idea of Yahweh transformed the Ten Commandments into a way of shaking people out of their habitual hang-ups.

Here is Jesus, then, confronted with a dilemma. If he says, "Don't stone her," he breaks the Law; if he says, "Stone her," then he is abandoning his own teaching. They keep urging him, "What is your answer?" He leans over and starts writing in the sand with his finger. How long this went on we don't know, but everybody was getting restless. What was he writing? What was he doing? Nobody really knew. Maybe he was simply passing the time of day, somewhat as students at a dull lecture doodle in their notebooks. Doodling is a gesture meaning, "I'm bored" or, "This discussion doesn't interest me."

His accusers were not about to let him out of the trap that they had so carefully fashioned. So they kept urging him, "Master, what is the solution to this difficult case?" At last he straightened up, looked around at those zealots of the Law and said, "Let the man who has no sin on his conscience throw the first stone." Then he bent down and continued to write in the sand.

Notice that he did not challenge their right to carry out the Law; he simply insisted on a condition: "Go ahead and throw stones provided you don't have any sin on your own conscience." They got the message and so the text significantly states, "One by one they began to leave beginning with the eldest."

As you get older, this business of salvation seems to become more and more elusive. The elder members of this group, with the experience of age, left right away, while the younger ones with their zeal got the message only by degrees. Finally, nobody was left except this woman and Jesus doodling in the sand.

At last he looked at her and, with the pointed irony that is so characteristic of some of Jesus' sayings, asked, "Where did everybody disappear to?" He knew perfectly well where they had gone. Perhaps he thought it somewhat humorous that their trap had been foiled by that statement of his. Then he asked, "Does anyone condemn you?" She said, "Nobody, sir." Notice she said "sir." She did not call him the Messiah or rabbi. She was honest. Since she did not have any faith, she just said, "sir," the way she might address any nice man. (The final words, "From now on avoid this sin," are probably a gloss by some pious copyist. Some of the platitudes that follow Jesus' parables sound unauthentic.)

Notice the respect Jesus has for this woman. He does not try to preach to her. He simply shows compassion by getting her out of the jam. He identifies with her in her humiliation. This is important for us to grasp in our own spiritual journey. Grace is the action and presence of Christ Jesus in our lives right now. As Christians we believe that, when the community is gathered for worship, Christ is truly present in his glorified body.

Jesus identifies with sinners not by sharing their sins, but by sharing the consequences of their sins. Jesus ate with public sinners. Having a meal in common in the culture of the time was the symbol of belonging to that group of people, family, or nation. That is why the Pharisees were so shocked when Jesus ate with sinners. He was identifying with the outcasts of society — not only with the oppressed who were unjustly rejected, but also with sinners who were rightly rejected. This means that just as Jesus identified with public sinners in the suffering that was the consequence of their sins, so he identifies with us in the sufferings that we endure because of our false self and our personal sins. We can unite ourselves to him in the full confidence that his mercy reaches out to the human misery that is the consequence of our personal sins. No matter how far we run from God, Christ is always there waiting for us. In the words of Abbé Huvelin, "Christ has so taken the lowest place that no one can take it from him."

The last point in this story is extremely interesting. It is another example of the teaching contained in the parable of the prodigal son. In that parable the father's love first takes care of the most obvious sinner, the prodigal. After we have heard about the father's great mercy toward that son, we hear about the self-righteous older son who had always behaved himself in a respectful and dutiful way. He turns out to be the bigger sinner, but the father shows him equal mercy.

In this story we see Jesus offering his great mercy to the sinful woman, but notice that the words with which he rescued her are an invitation to the accusers to enter into their own consciences and to see what is wrong with them. The trouble with self-righteous people is that they are just as much sinners as the people they condemn, only they do not know it. They are thus more difficult to help. When Jesus said, "Let the man without sin throw the first stone, "He is saying to the accusers, "How about looking into your own consciences?" He is asking, "What is your motive? Are you taking rightful responsibility for this act?"

God continues to love the oppressors as well as the oppressed. We will never be able to save the oppressed unless we have compassion on the oppressors. They also need salvation. This God of ours has no favorites; he is out to rescue everybody. Many oppressors have themselves been oppressed in early childhood.

The accusers of the woman thought they were upholding the Law; they did not recognize their hypocrisy in using the Law in order to entrap Jesus. He invited them to look into their consciences and face the pride that was motivating their malice. The basic question is always: What is your motive for this act? It is an invitation to conversion, to take full responsibility for ourselves, our community, nation, and religion. Jesus laid down his life for the human family. And it is by doing the same that we accept the call to follow him.

6

THE QUESTIONING OF PETER

When they had finished breakfast, Jesus said to Simon Peter, "Simon, son of John, do you love me more than these?" He said to him, "Yes, Lord, you know that I love you." He said to him, "Feed my lambs." He then said to him a second time, "Simon, son of John, do you love me?" He said to him, "Yes, Lord, you know that I love you." He said to him, "Tend my sheep." He said to him the third time, "Simon, son of John, do you love me?" Peter was distressed that he had said to him a third time, "Do you love me?" and he said to him, "Lord, you know everything; you know that I love you." [Jesus] said to him, "Feed my sheep. Amen, amen, I say to you, when you were younger, you used to dress yourself and go where you wanted; but when you grow old, you will stretch out your hands, and someone else will dress you and lead you where you do not want to go." He said this signifying by what kind of death he would glorify God. And when he had said this, he said to him, "Follow me."

(John 21:15–19)

This dialogue between Peter and Jesus took place on the shore of the Lake of Tiberias after a long night of fruitless fishing. John the Evangelist calls it the third appearance of Jesus.

It was on this occasion that the disciples, at the suggestion of the stranger on the beach, cast their nets to the other side of their boats and obtained a remarkable catch of 153 fish. When they arrived on the shore pulling their nets, they found that the stranger had provided them with breakfast. He called for some of the fish that they had caught and then invited them to eat.

This nostalgic scene tends to go on and on. After breakfast a dialogue takes place when Jesus invites Peter to walk with him along the beach. Peter had denied the Lord three times. His triple denial was lying heavily on his mind, the way our own failures lie heavily on our consciences. Having done something we wish we had not or not done something we wish we had, we have to live with the consequences. Every now and then we are confronted by some incident from our past life during prayer, and we have the sense that the Lord is taking us by the hand or putting his arm around us. Guilt feelings tend to make us think that he is staring at us with a severe glance as if to say, "You wretched so-and-so." But this is a projection of how *we* feel, not how God feels. In any case, Peter was feeling as if the finger were pointing at him as Jesus invited him for this heart-to-heart talk after breakfast. Notice the timing. It was not on an empty stomach. God picks the right moment for these searching confrontations.

Here then is the first question, "Simon, Son of John, do you love me?" Peter's internal "commentator" — the emotional judgment that assesses everything that happens — goes off. The "commentator" says, "Look, he's giving you the formal treatment." Simon, son of John, was a formal address suitable for a law court. Instead of calling him Peter, the name given him at their first meeting, Jesus substitutes the formal address that goes with heavy occasions, "Simon, son of John, do you love me?" Each one of these words is delicately nuanced, and unless we grasp these nuances, we will not perceive the extraordinary depth of this exchange and the excruciating nature of the interrogation. "Do you love me?" The word "love" in Greek is not translatable. It means "do you love me with the disinterested love that I have shown you?" or "do you love me with the self-giving love that seeks no reward?"

Peter's answer is, "Yes, Lord, you know that I love you." But Peter does not use the same word for "love" that Jesus did. Thus he does not lay claim to the kind of love that he has received. He simply says, "You know that I love you." Peter's word for "love" refers to brotherly love or the love of friendship. In other words, "You know I love you with my human affection (the way people normally love each other)."

Jesus says, "Feed my lambs."

They walk on a little farther while the implications of the first question percolate in Peter's conscience. Then comes a second question, "Simon, son of John, do you really love me?" Again Jesus uses the term for divine love or self-giving love.

Peter is aware of where these questions are going. All his pretensions that were prominent in his early discipleship, his desire to be the right-hand man of the Messiah, have crumbled. His three denials have laid bare who he really is. When the chips were down, so was he. There is no chance that Peter now lays claim to selfless love or to any depth of dedication. He is naked in front of the truth to which Jesus has lovingly brought him. So once again Peter says, "You know that I love you with my poor human affection." That is all he can lay claim to.

As they walk on, the questions are bringing Peter to a new depth of understanding. With the words, "Feed my sheep," Peter must be aware that Jesus is reinstating him as the chief of the apostles. He is also aware of the condition, which is his acknowledgment of his total dependence on Christ.

Now comes a third and final question. The other two had prepared Peter for this one. I doubt that he could have endured it without the other two going first. God does not ask us to face the full truth of our capacity for all evil right away. Here is the question, "Simon, son of John, do you really love me?" Jesus' word for "love" is not divine love (*agape*), the term he has been using, but the word that Peter has been using. The implication is, "Do you really love me as a brother or friend? Do you even love me with your human affection?" In other words, "Do you have any love for me at all?"

This question brings Peter's human love and affection for Jesus into doubt, and the doubt is being raised by the person who means everything to him. To put the question another way, "In the light of your behavior, Simon, son of John, I ask one final question. Do you love me at all?"

Here is Peter pleading with Jesus to believe in his human affection and Jesus asks, "Are you sure?"

Peter's answer is, "Lord, you know everything." The Greek word for "know" refers to divine knowledge. It is to Jesus as God that Peter appeals when he says, "You know everything." But in the next sentence the word for "know" changes. Peter appeals only to Jesus' human knowledge as he continues, "You know that I love you." To paraphrase Peter's words: "Can't you see, just by human observation, that I really love you?" Thus Peter lays no claim to the love that is the primary qualification for apostleship.

Jesus replies, "Feed my sheep." Jesus seems to say, "I accept your human affection, but I am calling you to perfect love which is to love as I have loved you." Thus Peter will receive the love which is *agape* now that he has acknowledged that it is sheer gift, and one day he will lay down his life for him.

Finally Jesus says to him, "Follow me." These are the same words that Jesus said to him when he first called him to be a disciple — the same words, and yet an infinite distance has been traversed in those few years, the distance between the presumption of Peter's false self and the humility of enlightened self-knowledge.

The love of Christ holds nothing against anybody, but it cannot penetrate the presumption of pride. The false self does not want to be transformed. It wants to hide everything negative about itself and pretend that it can run our lives and perhaps everybody else's.

Humility is the necessary condition for the proper exercise of authority in the church. When it is not present, nothing works. Since Peter was to be the chief shepherd, he had to be brought to the realization that everything was the sheer gift of the Lord. Only then was he ready to receive the Spirit and to be the head of the church. In those questions, Jesus lovingly hurls him from one abyss of humiliation to another while at the same time reaffirming him in his vocation.

These are the same questions we hear in the night of sense and still more in the night of spirit.

7

THE ULTIMATE EXPRESSION

"And just as Moses lifted up the serpent in the desert, so must the Son of Man be lifted up, so that everybody who believes in him may have eternal life." For God so loved the world that he gave his only Son, so that everybody who believes in him might not perish but might have eternal life. For God did not send his Son into the world to condemn the world, but that the world might be saved through him.

(John 3:14–17)

This text begins with the striking image of the brazen serpent described in Exodus which healed the poison that the Israelites had contracted from the plague of serpents. As they looked upon the brazen serpent raised on a stick, the healing took place. Jesus uses this example to predict his passion. The image is ghastly: a worm fixed to a stake squirming in pain.

This brings us to one of the most profound questions that the Gospel raises: What is Ultimate Reality? To manifest Ultimate Reality is the goal of the Buddhist religion and to manifest the Spirit is the goal of the Christian religion. This question might be brought into focus by juxtaposing two remarkable images from these two world religions. One is the Buddha sitting in deep *samadhi* with a smile of ineffable peace upon his lips.

There is a shrine in Sri Lanka that Thomas Merton visited just before his death and where he received what he describes in his *Asian Journal* as the crowning grace of his Asian trip. He had gone to the East to seek Asian wisdom in order to enhance his contemplative Christian journey. He received at that shrine a remarkable enlightenment experience. He saw epitomized in that work of art the ultimate human achievement and the full realization of enlightenment — the possession of all knowledge in perfect freedom, peace, and serenity — captured by the smile of ineffable peace. The smile was not one of indifference, but of utter compassion without emotional involvement. The face of the Buddha suggests how he looked during his last *samadhi* before entering into final Nirvana, the attainment of oneness with all that is. The delicate smile transmits the Buddha's experience of unity to his disciples.

Now let us look at the other image: Jesus dying on the cross, his lips contorted in the agony of thirst and suffocation. From those lips comes a cry of almost infinite despair, "My God, my God, why have you forsaken me?" "Me!" that is, "Your Son!" This is the ultimate double-bind: Jesus Christ, the Son of God, experiencing the uttermost alienation that anyone could ever experience.

Let us compare these two states, one of utmost serenity and the other of utmost suffering. These are, as far as we know, the states in which each of them died.

Which manifestation of God is greater? If these two human beings are both manifesting the Ultimate Reality in a supreme manner, then who is this God who can be expressed in two completely opposite ways? Each expresses the Ultimate Reality in a way that no other human expression could manifest. The mystery that we call God transcends every human experience but is clearly present in the marvelous serenity lingering on the lips of the Buddha. What we draw back from is that the same divine reality is equally present in the suffering Jesus epitomized as he endures every level of human privation. His rejection, humiliation, and death tell us something about God that nobody had ever heard of or imagined. Jesus, in taking upon himself the human condition and laying aside the divine prerogatives that he could have called upon, rejects the archetypes of immortality, invincibility, and invulnerability and refuses to call upon his divine power to rescue either himself or his mission. He manifests the ultimate humility of God: the desire not to be God. This total emptying, which is the heart of divine love, takes place forever in the Trinity as the Father and the Son empty themselves into each other in the love of the Spirit.

When divine love enters the human condition with the inevitable consequences of this union, it becomes total vulnerability. God is present not just in serenity, not just in spiritual achievement; God is also present in failure and the utmost suffering, and he manifests himself equally in each expression. Jesus' passion and death is the revelation of the heart of God. Jesus took upon himself all the consequences of the human condition, one of which is sin; he who knew not sin experienced the psychological consequences of alienation from God, which is the chief fruit of personal sin. This meant the loss of his perception of oneness with the Father, who was the whole meaning of his life and mission. The crucifixion was the destruction of his life's work, not just his life. Thus, the lips of Jesus, torn by suffering and expressing the sense of abandonment by the Divine Person who was closest to him, tells us that God is just as present in his absence as in his presence, in suffering as in glory.

This of course is not the end of the story. Though Jesus died with the ultimate question still on his lips, he moved into a new and inconceivable reality. The surrender of his personal union with the Father catapulted him into a state of being in which his very humanity becomes identified with the Godhead. He is in unity with the Father and with everything that exists. His glorified humanity shares the divine attributes. He is present everywhere, in everyone, in everything, and at the heart of all reality. He is the divine human being through whom everything returns to the Father.

8

THE FRUITS OF THE SPIRIT

Jesus returned to Galilee in the power of the Spirit, and news of him spread throughout the whole region. He taught in their synagogues and was praised by all. He came to Nazareth, where he had grown up, and went according to his custom into the synagogue on the Sabbath day. He stood up to read and was handed a scroll of the prophet Isaiah. He unrolled the scroll and found the passage where it was written:

> *"The Spirit of the Lord is upon me,*
> *because he has anointed me to bring glad tidings to*
> *the poor.*
> *He has sent me to proclaim liberty to captives*
> *and recovery of sight to the blind,*
> *to let the oppressed go free,*
> *and to proclaim a year acceptable to the Lord."*

Rolling up the scroll, he handed it back to the attendant and sat down, and the eyes of all in the synagogue looked intently at him. He said to them, "Today this scripture passage is been fulfilled in your hearing."

(Luke 4:14–21)

The purpose of the readings in the liturgy is not so much instruction as demonstrations of the power of grace. They are parables of the power of the grace as we experience it now. We are exposed in the liturgy to sapiential teaching, that is, teaching designed to awaken our awareness of the grace of Christ at work within us. As the liturgical community celebrates divine light and life, our participation presupposes that we are experiencing it. In the lessons we hear our own biographies.

At Christmas, we celebrate the event of the Word becoming flesh. The historical implications are predominant in that feast. At the Feast of Epiphany, which is the transmission of divine light, we are celebrating the spiritual significance of the Christmas event. Epiphany is the celebration of our union with the Word made flesh and our experience of that union. The liturgy presents us with readings that are historically disconnected but which describe our assimilation to the mystery of the Word made flesh, our awakening to the divine life within us and our capacity to transmit it. "Today" in the liturgy means the transmission of the mystery as immediate spiritual experience. The Christian religion is a life to be lived. It starts, falters, falls, rises, grows, and eventually matures through all kinds of vicissitudes. We must know how to listen to the liturgy not only as inspiration and encouragement, but also as empowerment.

The Second Coming of Christ can occur in two ways: with the end of time (only God knows when that is) or by our accessing the eternal dimension within us. The latter is what the liturgy and the spiritual journey are attempting to bring about. The values of eternal life are constantly breaking into the linear dimension of chronological time and putting us in contact with the Ultimate Reality.

The lessons of the liturgy following the Epiphany are about the significance of being incorporated into what Paul calls the body of Christ. In each moment of chronological time, the divine value of each moment is available to us in proportion to our sensitivity to the Spirit of Christ. The Spirit suggests what is to be done at each moment in our relationship to God, ourselves, other people, and the cosmos. When we listen to the movements of the Spirit rather than to our own bright ideas and self-centered programs for happiness, the internal commentary that normally sustains our emotional upsets comes to an end, enabling us to accept difficult situations and people. The neutral zone that we provide allows the Spirit to act.

Notice Jesus was led by the Spirit to Nazareth. He did not go there of his own initiative. He was following a movement of the Spirit within him with whom he was totally identified. God is infinite concern for every living thing. That is the source of every true mission or ministry in the church. It is not our work. It a movement of love in the Trinity. The liturgy is the great means of awakening and empowering us to be who we are: living cells in the Body of Christ, motivated by the same love that we see in Jesus.

9

CURE OF THE BLIND MAN

They came to Jericho. And as he was leaving Jericho with his disciples and a sizable crowd, Bartimaeus, a blind man, the son of Timaeus, sat by the roadside begging. On hearing that it was Jesus of Nazareth, he began to cry out and say, "Jesus, Son of David, have pity on me." And many rebuked him, telling him to be silent. But he kept calling out all the more, "Son of David, have pity on me." Jesus stopped and said, "Call him." So they called the blind man, saying to him, "Take courage; get up, he is calling you." He threw aside his cloak, sprang up, and came to Jesus. Jesus said to him in reply, "What do you want me to do for you?" The blind man replied to him, "Master, I want to see." Jesus told him, "Go your way; your faith has saved you." Immediately he received his sight and followed him on the way.

(Mark 10:46–52)

All of the Gospel texts that speak of the healing of the afflictions of the body point to the interior change that Jesus was able to communicate on the spiritual level. Without that healing, one is blind to spiritual reality, deaf to the word of God. We see only the superficial level of reality and hear only what the ears take in. Neither awakens the intuitive faculties that perceive the inner nature of reality and the mystery within the symbols

37

of the liturgy. The ultimate message of the universe is not enjoyed because it is not perceived. We are stuck on the external level of things.

This is the basic problem that religious practices are designed to heal. Jesus' disciples had as much trouble as we have. At the Last Supper, Philip asked Jesus to show them the Father, the Abba whom Jesus had been talking about all during his public life. Jesus was a little put out by this question and responded, "Philip, have I been with you for so long a time and you still don't know me? One who sees me sees the Father!" This seeing is certainly not with the bodily eyes. Only the X-ray eyes of faith penetrate the surface of skin and bones. We get stuck on a person's personality, ethnic background, nationality, life style, or religious commitment — things that prevent us from touching the beauty of the person regardless of things that might put us off. Neither did the disciples hear well. Jesus said again and again, "If you have ears to hear, hear!" implying that they were listening to his words but not listening to the inner reality his words were pointing to.

The blind man had heard of Jesus of Nazareth while begging for the necessities of life. When Jesus comes by on the road along with a great multitude, he starts shouting. Jesus hears his cry and says, "Bring the man here."

The sense of being called is translated into our experience by the attraction to the spiritual journey, and to the service of others out of a motivation of genuine concern. All the basic human values reflect a hunger for the true happiness that is everyone's potential and that can be activated when we see with the eyes of faith or hear with the ears of hope.

Spiritual awakening can be described in terms of the spiritual senses. When we hear about Jesus healing the sick in the Gospel, we must be alert to the fact that he is healing their spiritual blindness, lameness, muteness, or deafness. The devil flying out of people in Jesus' time signifies the release of their addictions and compulsions. The healing of leprosy symbolized the healing of the false self because in those days leprosy meant certain death; indeed it involved a social death even while one was physically alive.

The first manifestation of the spiritual senses is the attraction for God. It can be simply an attraction to be alone with him, silent, still. It is a certain dissatisfaction with thinking about God or just talking to him. Jesus said, "The kingdom of heaven is close." Translated into the spiritual senses, this wisdom saying points to the interior sense of God's presence. It dislodges the monumental illusion that God is far away because we do not feel him.

Touch is a more developed spiritual sense, a further insight into how close God actually is to us.

"The kingdom of God is within you" corresponds to the sense of taste. This spiritual sense perceives that God is not just close to us, but that we are rooted in him. The food we eat is taken inside of us and becomes us through its transformation into cells in our body. In a sense, we become what we eat. In the transcendent relationship, we become cells in the Body of Christ, the new humanity whose eyes and ears are opening to reality at its deepest level.

The spiritual sense of smell symbolizes the attraction toward God; touch symbolizes the closeness of God; and taste symbolizes the sense of oneness with God. When we see with the eyes of faith and hear with the ears of hope, we become responsive to what the gospel is saying. Without that awakening, we are constantly blown around by our surface impressions and emotional reactions to life. The development of the spiritual senses puts us directly in touch with the divine wisdom which evaluates things from God's point of view.

The spiritual senses are like external senses because of their immediacy. They put us in touch with the reality not through the external senses, but through the intuitive faculties that directly perceive the greater values of the universe. These can be gradually awakened through contemplative prayer. The awakening of the spiritual senses is the call of the gospel to see with the eyes of faith. When the spiritual senses are activated, then we truly hear, then we truly see; we have the receptive apparatus to open to the heart of reality. Through faith, hope, and charity we hear the ultimate message of the universe. The result of that awakening is symbolized in what the blind man did on receiving his sight: he followed him.

Jesus emphasizes what healed him. Faith! This was not just the faith that works through reason, but the faith that is a direct intuition. "Go in peace," he says to this man, "your faith has saved you." Your faith, that is, your consent to God calling you, touching you, transforming you. Transformation in Christ is the ultimate healing.

10

PRODIGAL SON

Then he said, "A man had two sons, and the younger son said to his father, 'Father, give me the share of your estate that should come to me.' So the father divided the property between them. After a few days, the younger son collected all his belongings and set off to a distant country where he squandered his inheritance in a life of dissipation. When he had freely spent everything, a severe famine struck that country, and he found himself in dire need. So he hired himself out to one of the local citizens who sent him to his farm to tend the swine. And he longed to eat his fill of the pods on which the swine fed, but nobody gave him any. Coming to his senses he thought, 'How many of my father's hired workers have more than enough food to eat, but here am I, dying from hunger. I shall get up and go to my father and I shall say to him, "Father, I have sinned against heaven and against you. I no longer deserve to be called your son; treat me as you would treat one of your hired workers."' So he got up and went back to his father. While he was still a long way off, his father caught sight of him, and was filled with compassion. He ran to his son, embraced him and kissed him. His son said to him, 'Father, I have sinned against heaven and against you; I no longer deserve to be called your son.' But his father ordered his servants, 'Quickly bring the finest

*robe and put it on him; put a ring on his fingers and sandals
on his feet. Take the fattened calf and slaughter it. Then let
us celebrate with a feast, because this son of mine was dead,
and has come to life again; he was lost, and has been found.'
Then the celebration began."*

(Luke 15:11–24)

Here we see a young man who obviously has an enormous
emotional investment in having a good time. He had been saving up his money and now has the inheritance he asked for. His
drive for happiness centers around pleasure, affection, and esteem. So he gathers his possessions and heads off for the good
life. While he is out on his prolonged toot, his emotional program for pleasure does not work out as well as expected. In the
midst of his enjoyment of the high life comes a great famine; he
loses all his money, his friends desert him, and he has nothing
to eat. Out of desperation he takes the job of herdsman in a
pigsty. In the local culture this was the lowest form of earning
a living. At this point, he remembers how well fed everybody
was at home including the hired servants. Notice that his motive for going home was not the best. His chief reason is that his
program for happiness based on pleasure was not viable.

This parable communicates the fact that we are relating with
a God who is infinitely concerned. The father of the prodigal
was waiting for years for his son to wake up and realize that
happiness is not to be found in the pursuit of pleasure. When
he sees his son heading home, he is deeply moved. In fact, he is
so touched by the sight of this bedraggled child on his way home
that he forgets about the shabby way the boy had treated him
when he went off with his share of the inheritance. He rushes
out to meet him and heaps all kinds of welcome on him.

This parable is addressed to people who are living a life that
the general public regards as disreputable. Most sinners, at a
deep level, are insecure, lonely, and usually acting out the damage done to them in early life. Their actual conduct is not so

much their choice as the result of desperate attempts to deal with the overwhelming emotional trauma inflicted on them by adults at an age when they could not handle it. This father's one concern is to reinstate his son. The son's hope is to get a position among the hired hands where he would get enough to eat. That is the extent of his trust in his father. The reception he received must have come as a shock to him. He suddenly realizes that he has never understood his father or the extent of his father's love for him, never fathomed his father's concern and depth of forgiveness.

This parable is aimed at the hearts of people who have lost hope and whose despair is expressed in the constant repetition of lifestyles that cannot bring happiness. Yet they are locked into them because they do not know the happiness found in God's friendship that would pull them out of the vicious circle of desire, gratification, and frustration — the endless cycle of craving and disappointment. The father was ready to forgive and forget everything in his delight in finding the son who was lost. Going into a far country in search of happiness was a tragedy because true security, independence, and affection were all present in his father's house and the prodigal son did not know it.

The sinners who are listening to Jesus are being invited into the same boundless forgiveness. It is not merit that brings one into the friendship of this father but consent to his infinite goodness and concern.

What do we do after we have come home, after we have chosen once again to live under the gaze of God's infinite tenderness instead of hiding from it? What do we do with feelings of greed, pride, vainglory, jealousy, envy, lust, wanting to manipulate other people, or in short, with the whole world of selfishness that does not belong in the father's house?

This return to the father's house is not the return to heaven. It is only a return to the right orientation of our lives with all the damage that we bring with us from early childhood. Once we have chosen the orientation of living in the father's house, the symbol of God's presence, Jesus joins us wherever we are. The acts of selfishness, backward glances, regressive tendencies to former emotional states are all something that we share with Christ and he with us. He identifies with our personal history in every detail. Instead of thinking we are alienated from God when afflictive emotions arise, we realize that they are fuel for divine love. We can then welcome them without identifying with them because we see them as wounds that God is trying to heal.

In this story nothing is said about the boy's mother. The father seems to be a single parent, both mother and father to his sons. Perhaps the mother's absence was the boy's basic problem from the moment he started out in life. Our mother is our first window onto God, and if this window is missing because of misunderstandings, physical absence, or inadequate parenting, the window is hard to open later in life. The vocation of a mother must be one of the greatest vocations there is. Starting out well in life would solve an enormous number of problems.

11

THE HIDDEN GOD

About eight days after he said this, he took Peter, John and James and went up the mountain to pray. While he was praying, his face changed in appearance and his clothing became dazzlingly white. And behold, two men were conversing with him, Moses and Elijah, who appeared in glory and spoke of his exodus that he was going to accomplish in Jerusalem. Peter and his companions had been overcome by sleep, but becoming fully awake, they saw his glory and the two men standing with him. As they were about to depart from him, Peter said to Jesus, "Master, it is good that we are here; let us make three tents, one for you, one for Moses, and one for Elijah." But he did not know what he was saying. While he was still speaking, a cloud came and cast a shadow over them, and they became frightened when they entered the cloud. Then from the cloud came a voice that said, "This is my chosen Son; listen to him." After the voice had spoken, Jesus was found alone. They fell silent and did not at that time tell anyone what they had seen.

(Luke 9:28–36)

This text has always exercised a great appeal for contemplatives from both East and West. Notice the key words that apply to contemplative prayer. *Listening* is the chief work of contemplative prayer. It is a steppingstone or diving board into the spiritual level of our being. Notice also that *a cloud overshadowed them.* A cloud is a favorite image of God's presence beyond concepts. The apostles *wake up and are enlightened.* There is also talk of *sleep,* not an infrequent companion of contemplatives during prayer.

Jesus, the son of God, emptied himself in order to enter the human family. The dazzling glory that poured out from every pore of his body and transfigured his clothes is coming from a power that was always present in him, but normally well hidden. This is one of the few occasions in which he allowed his ordinary glory to come through and manifest itself. If Moses had to veil his face after conversing with God, what would the son of God have had to do in order not to frighten people away? Jesus' emptying is the letting go of his divine prerogatives in-so-far as these could be manifested in a human being. This event is one of the great mysteries of faith comparable to Christmas, Epiphany, Easter, and Pentecost.

Notice the three disciples whom he brings with him to the mountain. You might be inclined to say, "Lucky guys! They were worthy, I suppose, to go." But take a look at their resumes. Peter aspired to be the right-hand man of the Messiah. He got what he wanted but not until he had been through the threshing floor of humiliation. As for James and John, they were just one step away from being terrorists. They wanted to bring down fire from heaven and destroy the Samaritan towns that were inhospitable, the equivalent of dropping an atomic bomb on them.

So do not exclude yourself from this invitation. In the persons of the disciples with their long list of human failings, everybody is invited to the holy mountain. Everybody is invited to experience the transfiguration, to enter the cloud, to hear the voice of God, to share the silence that fell upon them, and to tremble with their fear. Their fear was not the emotion of fear that separates from God or prompts one to run away, but rather the awesome fascination of the mystery that draws one irresistibly into the cloud and that longs to touch and taste the mystery that is hidden in the darkness. Contemplative prayer accesses God in a darkness that is luminous and enlivening; it is not just a blank, a trance or deep sleep.

If the divinity of Christ is hidden in Jesus in such a way that no one saw it except on the occasion of the transfiguration, how much more can it be hidden but truly present in those who participate in Christ's life through faith?

The grace of the transfiguration is the radiance of Christ's hidden presence in us. Let us see how this works out in our experience. We also are entering the cloud. We also are listening to Jesus at the command of the Father. Peter wanted to stay there for good. "Let's camp here," he said, "and build a booth for Moses, Elijah, and for Jesus." Peter's hospitality greatly exceeded his authority; he did not own the mountain. His words express his desire to continue to enjoy the pleasure of the moment. When contemplative prayer is consoling, peaceful, meaningful, radiant, the false self quickly identifies with this delightful situation and wants it to go on forever. The point to keep in mind is that the divine energy is just as present (as it was in Jesus' ordinary life) when it is not perceived. When God's gracious goodness overflows or radiates for a few moments, hours, or days, this does not mean that consolation is all there is to contemplation. What we feel is our own interpretation, not the essence of the mystery.

Just as the apostles were always in Jesus' presence as they toured Galilee, we too are always in his presence. But the perception of his presence is reserved to special moments. Mature contemplatives of all times have identified the transfiguration as one of them. We participate in the transfiguration by the experience of spiritual consolation. But we must not let the false self try to hang on to this exuberant gift unduly. Having appreciated and enjoyed it, we must allow the prophets to go back to where they came from, Jesus to come down from the mountain, and ourselves to return to the humdrum events of everyday life and to our accustomed state of prayer, which by any standard is usually a mess. The mess effectively hides the divine presence just as the sacred humanity of Jesus — his body, his dirty feet, and unruly beard — hid his divinity. Jesus was no prize package to behold during his ministry and especially not during his passion and death. Similarly, daily life is Jesus hidden in our ups and downs, under the appearance of unwanted thoughts, the unloading of the unconscious, and the spasms of pride and lust. The divine action is always present, but our faculties perceive it only when the grace of the transfiguration is infused into us. We should think of prayer primarily as our participation in the passion and death of Jesus. The resurrection does not come first. It comes after we share in his passion, too late to make the spiritual journey an easy trip, but at just the right time from the point of view of humbling the incredible pride of the human species.

Once we commit ourselves to the journey, we have to shake off our expectations and mind sets and allow God to be God in us. We plug into the divine energy by consent, not by feeling or experience. This energy is totally available all the time on one condition — the consent of faith. Out of that faith comes the power to surrender to the work of transformation. The grace of the resurrection, manifested in us by the fruits of the Spirit, is not consolation; it is the strength that comes from being rooted in Christ by faith beyond feelings, concepts, or any experience, however spiritual.

12

THE PENITENT WOMAN

A Pharisee invited him to dine with him, and he entered the Pharisee's house and reclined at table. Now there was a sinful woman in the city who learned that he was at table in the house of the Pharisee. Bringing an alabaster flask of ointment, she stood behind him at his feet weeping and began to bathe his feet with her tears. Then she wiped them with her hair, kissed them, and anointed them with the ointment. When the Pharisee who had invited him saw this he said to himself, "If this man were a prophet, he would know who and what sort of woman this is who is touching him, that she is a sinner." Jesus said to him in reply, "Simon, I have something to say to you." "Tell me, teacher," he said. "Two people were in debt to a certain creditor; one owed five hundred days' wages and the other owed fifty. Since they were unable to repay the debt, he forgave it for both. Which of them will love him more?" Simon said in reply, "The one, I suppose, whose larger debt was forgiven." He said to him, "You have judged rightly." Then he turned to the woman and said to Simon, "Do you see this woman? When I entered your house, you did not give me water for my feet, but she has bathed them with her tears and wiped them with her hair. You did not give me a kiss, but she has not ceased kissing my feet since the time I entered. You did not anoint

my head with oil, but she anointed my feet with ointment.
So I tell you, her many sins have been forgiven; hence, she
has shown great love. But the one to whom little is forgiven,
loves little." He said to her, "Your sins are forgiven." The
others at table said to themselves, "Who is this who even
forgives sins?" But he said to the woman, "Your faith has
saved you; go in peace."

(Luke 7:36–50)

This impressive story is one of the most important along with
the parables of the prodigal son, the woman taken in adultery,
the lost coin, the lost sheep, and the good thief. Let us try to
understand the precise point that Jesus is making in this episode.

It seems that he accepted an invitation to a formal dinner
at the Pharisee's house. While everybody was reclining, as was
the custom then, and ingesting the delicious meal, an uninvited
guest suddenly appeared. A woman who had a shady reputation
entered and stood behind Jesus as he was reclining. She started
sobbing. Surrendering to an impulse, she rained her tears on his
feet and dried them with her hair. Next she produced a bottle
of perfume and poured its odoriferous contents over his feet.

It is important to recall that a distinguished guest in those
days always received water to wash his feet, a kiss of welcome
on the cheek and ointment for his head. The Pharisee had per-
formed none of these customary services. Thus, in actual fact, he
had insulted Jesus. Apparently, the woman was not aware of this
lack of even the ordinary courtesies and was simply following
an impulse of the Spirit.

In any case, the woman was acting in a way that was, by
any standard, mind-blowing. The embarrassment she caused
the Pharisee must have been considerable. Suppose during a
eucharistic celebration, as we were preparing for the offertory
at the sacred liturgy, a well-known male stripper appeared clad
in swimming trunks. Suppose he then burst into loud sobbing,
charged down the center aisle, and prostrated himself in front of

the altar with his nose to the ground. Everybody would feel that the offertory was not an appropriate time for such behavior.

This text has a similar scenario. The Pharisee considered the woman's behavior inappropriate conduct at a banquet and so it was not surprising that he had negative thoughts. Jesus, reading his mind and perhaps recalling that he had not provided any of the ordinary courtesies, was moved by the Spirit to reach out to this man. Jesus usually has a hidden agenda. He is not quick to judge the external conduct of others. At the same time, he reaches out in a subtle way to those who are oppressive or self-righteous and invites them to enter into themselves and perceive their own sinfulness. Motivation is Jesus' chief concern — *why* something is done rather than *what* is being done.

In this scene, Jesus compares the conduct of the Pharisee with the conduct of the woman. The basis for the comparison is the ordinary courtesies expected of a host. He points out that the Pharisee did not provide the courtesy of washing his feet, whereas the woman is bathing them with her tears. Jesus continues, "You did not anoint my head with oil and she is anointing my feet with perfume; you did not give me a kiss of welcome and she is kissing my feet." And he concludes, "Because of her great love, her sins have been forgiven." To paraphrase, "Based on the evidence of her love, her sins must have been forgiven. Based on the evidence of your conduct, which was to show no love at all, you must still be in your sins."

The Pharisee is not even aware that he needs forgiveness. Since he does not entrust himself to the divine mercy, he does not have the experience of being forgiven. That is the only experience that enables one to show great gratitude and love. Thus, to the astonishment of all, the person everybody spontaneously rejects, emerges as the hero, while the respectable Pharisee, manifesting attitudes proper to the social customs of the time, is implicitly accused of being a sinner.

The first part of the parable, then, warns us not to judge anyone by appearances alone. Perhaps it also raises a subtle question for the congregations who hear this text proclaimed, "And what are *you* doing, my dear Christians, to show love?" Those who have been forgiven much manifest it by the kind of love that they show.

Finally Jesus turns to the woman and, "Your sins are forgiven." This statement distresses the people at table and they whisper to each other, "Who does he think he is, forgiving sins?"

Their commentary is obviously a form of denial, a way of avoiding entering into themselves and evaluating where they are coming from. Jesus says to the woman, "Your faith has saved you." Her heart has been changed. It takes time for appropriate conduct to catch up with her new motivation. Appropriate conduct without the right motivation is Pharisaism, the occupational hazard of religious persons. Jesus constantly warns against it. He frequently highlights the pretensions of religious persons who are acting out of self-centered intentions. He does not care who we are or where we are coming from. Good will is all that he is interested in.

"Your faith has saved you," Jesus said. Faith in what? Faith in the divine goodness that is ready to forgive everything and everyone. Faith in the infinite mercy of God which is not concerned with numbers, since it is infinite, but with gratitude and self-surrender. By entrusting herself to divine love she received complete forgiveness and was empowered to prove her gratitude by the extent of her courtesy. Of course it was exaggerated. It had to be. Convention cannot provide the symbols to express gratitude which is that profound or extensive. Such love has to make a fool of itself. She does not seem to have been the least bit self-conscious about being in the wrong place or that it was inappropriate to provide such extraordinary courtesies. This is what impressed Jesus so much.

The bottom line of the second part of the story is an exhortation to entrust ourselves to the infinite mercy of God whether the number of our sins is many or few. The Pharisee's problem was that he was unaware that he needed to be forgiven. He was leading a respectable life and carrying out the Law. But because he was unaware of his need of forgiveness, he could not entrust himself to the mercy of God and be forgiven. Hence, he could not show the degree of love and gratitude that the penitent woman displayed. Jesus invites him to enter into his conscience and ask himself where he is really coming from. Those who are not aware of their need for forgiveness are in tough shape. It does not mean one has to be a great sinner because, as Jesus points out in the parable, neither of the debtors had the money to pay. Even if our sins are few, we do not have any way of paying our debt. Hence, the numbers are not important. What makes the difference is the degree to which we entrust ourselves to the mercy of God.

Actually, personal sin is not the problem in the first place. It is the false self with its orientation to prefer ourselves to others, including God. Out of that diseased root comes all the rotten fruit that the false self produces. Whether a bad tree produces a lot of apples or only a few, all the fruit is inedible. So we have to entrust the whole tree, root and branches, to the mercy of God who alone can heal the radical distortion of the human condition. This is what conversion is. It is not a Band-Aid approach to life. It is the radical letting go of our programs for self-centered happiness in the form of personal or collective security, power and control over others, and unlimited pleasure, affection and esteem. That is the sickness. That is the root of the diseased tree. To heal the disease requires a conversion as deep as that manifested by the penitent woman. Penitence is the disposition that is ready to give up the orientation of the false self and the pursuit of happiness based on the self-centered programs that trample on the rights and needs of others when they get in our way.

"Your faith has saved you." Faith means trust in the infinite mercy of God manifested in the redemptive work of Jesus. This is what saved the penitent woman; it can save each of us.

13

THE GREAT COMMANDMENT

One of the scribes, when he came forward and heard them disputing and saw how well he had answered them, asked him, "Which is the first of all the commandments?" Jesus replied, "The first is this: 'Hear O Israel! The Lord our God is Lord alone! You shall love the Lord your God with all your heart, with all your soul, with all your mind, and with all your strength.' The second is this: 'You shall love your neighbor as yourself.' There is no other commandment greater than these." The scribe said to him, "Well said, teacher. You are right in saying, He is One and there is no other than he.' And 'to love him with your heart, with all your understanding, with all your strength, and to love your neighbor as yourself' is worth more than all burnt offerings and sacrifices." And when Jesus saw that [he] answered with understanding, he said to him, "You are not far from the kingdom of God." And no one had the courage to ask him any more questions.

(Mark 12:28–34)

How can we possibly love the Lord with all our heart, soul, mind, and strength unless the false self has been significantly dismantled? If our strength is divided by all kinds of desires, this commandment is impossible. In any case, it is not something we start to observe on the first day of our conversion. It presupposes a process of liberation from selfishness. To be more specific, we cannot exercise the love of God emotionally, mentally, and spiritually, as this commandment demands, while under the influence of the emotional programs for happiness. For example, on the first rung of human consciousness, to feel secure is the chief concern. In the first year of life, consciousness is chiefly concerned with the ever-recurring round of desires and gratifications surrounding food, drink, shelter, and concrete signs of affection.

As we move on to year two or three, pleasure, affection and esteem, and control also become primary focuses of desire. From four to seven acceptance by family and peers is foremost in our value system.

As we evolve to the rational level with its capacity to climb out of the childish programs for happiness, reason tends to be dominated by the programs already in place. The word of God has to come into our hearts to touch us with the determination to dismantle the emotional programs for happiness, over identification with our group and the false self that was built up during early childhood. God graciously comes to our aid and begins to show us the basic selfishness of each of those programs and invites us to acknowledge them and to give them to him to take away. All of the afflictive emotions are rooted in the false self, and all of them begin to disappear once the values of the gospel that lead to true happiness are firmly established.

What Jesus is saying to this young scribe is that his abstract understanding of the primary precept of the Old Testament is "right on" and that if he pursues that course, the values of the false-self system are gradually freed from their fascination with pleasure, power, and security. One then moves into the awareness of the presence of God within. With that movement comes the capacity to love God with our whole mind, heart, soul and strength. By accessing the mystery of God's presence within, we are capable of perceiving the presence of God in others. The presence of God in us recognizes the presence of God in everyone else. Then it is possible to love them as ourselves.

The second precept flows automatically from the first. If we truly love God, we can love our neighbor as we love the true self that we have found through the process of liberation. The whole movement from the tyranny of Egypt to the promised land in the book of Exodus is a parable of the movement from the tyranny of the false self through the desert of purification into the promised land of interior freedom.

There is an intriguing second section to this text. Although Jesus approved of the first commandment and its corollary to love one's neighbor as oneself and congratulated the young man on his insight, he also said, "You are not far from the kingdom of God." In other words, the kingdom of God requires something more than to love our neighbor as ourselves. To love our neighbor from the perspective of the true self, as one possessing the image of God, is a great insight, but it still is not the fullness of the kingdom of God according to Jesus. A new commandment characterizes the Christian faith which carries the insight of the scribe a step further. It is to love one another *as Jesus has loved us*. This is much more difficult. This is to love others in their individuality, uniqueness, personality traits, temperamental biases, personal history, and in the things that drive us up the wall, to love our neighbor, in other words, just as they are with each one's grocery list of faults, unbearable habits, unreasonable demands, and impossible characteristics. The new commandment is to accept others unconditionally; that is to say, without the least wish to change them. To love them in their individuality is the way Jesus has loved us. He gives us the space in which to change and the time to confront the obstacles that prevent further change.

There are actually two approaches. One is to deliberately dismantle the emotional programs for happiness as we see them at work in our lives. A further practice and one that needs to be applied at the same time is the positive precept of unconditional love. This is the ascesis that Jesus himself suggests as the best way of dismantling the false self. It is to show untiring love beginning with the people that we live with and those who depend on us in one way or another. Jesus extended this ascesis to personal insult, injury, persecution, and even to death itself. This is the commandment that manifests whether or not we are fully in the kingdom. To be in the kingdom means to be at the disposal of the divine presence and action and to continue Christ's revelation in the world by how we live. This is the insight that was missing in the young scribe; it is the insight that Jesus gave to his disciples as his final will and testament. By exercising unconditional love, the dismantling of the false self takes place. This love is what Saint Augustine calls "bearing the unbearable." This is the mature Christian practice that is not put off by anything. By showing love unwearyingly, no matter what happens, we imitate and pass on the mercy that Christ has shown for us.

14

OUR LADY OF SORROWS

Standing by the cross of Jesus were his mother and his mother's sister, Mary the wife of Clopas, and Mary Magdala. When Jesus saw his mother and the disciple there whom he loved, he said to his mother, "Woman, behold, your son." Then he said to the disciple, "Behold your mother." And from that hour the disciple took her into his home.

(John 19:25–27)

The incidents in the Gospel of John have a significance far beyond the literal events that are described. Thus the words that Jesus spoke on the cross have meaning beyond his obvious concern about who was going to take care of his mother after his death. Christian tradition has developed the idea of the mother of Jesus as the new Eve, his companion in the monumental work of redemption and the opening of human awareness to unlimited growth. Mary has a close relationship to our own inner growth toward the full awareness of the Ultimate Reality. She is mother of the new humanity, the new creation that the gospel invites us to join and into which the sacrifice of Jesus initiates us. Mary has a special significance for contemplatives who are deliberately seeking to enter into this consciousness.

The Spirit of God penetrates us in somewhat the way the

human soul penetrates every cell in the body. In virtue of baptism and the gift of faith, the program of the body of Christ is coded within each of us. Our intuitive faculties are freed from the limitations of the senses and reasoning not by rejecting them, but by going beyond them and opening to the intuitive level of consciousness. The stages of contemplative prayer are levels of assimilation to the risen life of Christ. We put our human life, uniqueness, and talents into the transcendent project of manifesting God and transforming the present world into the new creation. Mary's intimate relationship with Christ, her disposition of self-surrender, her alert receptivity, and her promptness in responding to the wishes of the Spirit are the great contemplative virtues.

Standing beside the cross, she participated in the inauguration of the new creation. The apostles were wiped out in the face of Christ's crucifixion. John alone remained, though at a good distance; all the others left the scene and fled. The human props of their faith disappeared when Jesus was no longer cheered by the multitudes. When he was rejected by the ecclesiastical and civil authorities, the apostles were devastated. Their faith was dependent on human supports. When these were gone, so were they.

Mary, however, stayed by the cross. Her faith was not extinguished. The apostles saw Jesus as the Messiah but were not clear about his divinity. Mary was as clear as crystal about it. If they beheld Christ's destruction as the end of everything, what must she have felt when she looked upon Jesus not merely as the Messiah, but as God himself? The Eternal Word is the person whom she knew as her son. For her, God was dying, so to speak. The death of God was never so poignant a human experience as for her. This is the sword that pierced her heart. She was grieving not only for her son and for the Messiah; she was grieving for God. Only she perceived the depth of the mystery of the cross, of God throwing himself away, so to speak, for the salvation of insensitive and ungrateful people.

Mary is the paradigm of those who are manifesting Christ in their individual lives. Her compassion was rooted in the kind of love that God has for us — a love that is tender, firm, and completely self-giving. God-consciousness is the fruit of Christ's passion, death, resurrection, and ascension. In the ascension Jesus enters with his humanity into the heart of all creation where he dwells everywhere and in everything, visible only to the X-ray eyes of faith that penetrate through every disguise including the greatest of sorrows. God is reigning despite all appearances to the contrary. The risen Christ is ever-present, opening the way for the final triumph of God in which, as Paul says, "God will be all in all." This is the faith that Mary had when she looked on what was left of the flesh of her son and yet saw him reigning from the cross — the triumph of God hidden in the greatest suffering. This makes her our companion and support in every conceivable trial.

15

CHRIST THE KING

The people stood by and watched; the rulers, meanwhile, sneered at him and said, "He saved others, let him save himself if he is the chosen one, the Messiah of God." Even the soldiers jeered at him. As they approached to offer him wine they called out, "If you are the King of the Jews, save yourself." Above him there was an inscription that read, "This is the King of the Jews."

Now one of the criminals hanging there reviled Jesus, saying, "Are you not the Messiah? Save yourself and us." The other, however, rebuking him, said in reply, "Have you no fear of God, for you are subject to the same condemnation? And indeed, we have been condemned justly, for the sentence we received corresponds to our crimes, but this man has done nothing criminal." Then he said, "Jesus, remember me when you come into your kingdom." He replied to him, "Amen, I say to you, today you will be with me in Paradise."

(Luke 23:35–43)

The crucifixion of Jesus is the ultimate reversal of values. Jesus in the parables puts a tremor under the values of the people of his time. He continues to do the same for us as we hear the gospel today. He creates earthquakes under our self-satisfied

61

and prepackaged value systems. Here we see Jesus dying on the cross, crucified, rejected, obliterated, his life's work reduced to zero. In what does this reversal of values consist? It consists in divine love manifesting itself in the promise of Christ to the good thief. As soon as he opened to divine love, the thief ceased to be a thief. Jesus instantly acknowledged him as a member of the kingdom: "Today you will be with me in paradise."

The Pharisees and the Roman authorities were unrepentant. The good thief, by acknowledging his crime, ascended to heaven. This is the ultimate reversal of values. It is the confrontation of divine love and human pride.

John's Gospel perceives Jesus reigning from the cross. Divine love is triumphing over the apparent victory of worldliness, violence, and sin. Anyone who accepts that vision is reigning with Christ in the kingdom right now. To paraphrase Jesus' words to the good thief, "You are in paradise right now even amidst your sufferings." Thus, as soon as we open ourselves to divine love, our sins are forgiven and forgotten. We are instantly placed, like the good thief, in the reign of divine love. Thus, as the value systems of this world are reversed and selfishness is crucified in the body of Christ, divine love is poured out over the human family and made available to everyone who consents.

The reign of Christ the King is not a reign of power but of compassion. He invites us to participate.

16

THE PARTY IN MATTHEW'S HOUSE

As Jesus passed on from there, he saw a man named Matthew sitting at the customs post. He said to him, "Follow me." And he got up and followed him. While he was at table in his house, many tax collectors and sinners came and sat with Jesus and his disciples. The Pharisees saw this and said to his disciples, "Why does your teacher eat with tax collectors and sinners?" He heard this and said, "Those who are well do not need a physician, but the sick do. Go and learn the meaning of the words, 'I desire mercy, not sacrifice.' I did not come to call the righteous but sinners."
(Matt. 9:9–13)

The Gospel presents various responses to the coming of the kingdom of God in the person of Jesus Christ. This text provides another interesting response. Jesus was walking along and saw a man named Matthew at his post where the taxes were collected. Most of these tax collectors in those days were extortioners, and without accusing the eminent evangelist of having been a former crook, the chances are good that he was one. At least, he was fond of handling money, a significant problem for anyone's spiritual life.

Matthew upon being invited to be a disciple immediately

got up and followed Jesus. Notice the reversal of social expectations. The scribes and Pharisees were hanging back and trying to find ways of tripping up Jesus in speech. Matthew responded instantly to the call and seems to be the only disciple who did. The others all spent time with Jesus before they finally made the commitment.

Matthew was so happy about his conversion that he threw a party in his house and invited all his disreputable friends. So we read, "Many tax collectors and those known as sinners came to join Jesus and his disciples at dinner." This is a strange crowd for the son of God to be joining, but I guess the judgment depends on your attitude and where you are coming from. By sinners are probably meant the local male and female prostitutes. Imagine going into a fast-food place and finding Jesus sitting at a table in the back surrounded by the local prostitutes, gamblers, junkies, bums and extortioners.

Jesus seems to be quite at home in the house of Matthew, more so than in the house of the Pharisee. Some of the Pharisees observed that Jesus and his disciples were having a bash and started to complain: "What reason can the teacher have for eating with these crooks and others who disregard the Law?"

Jesus overheard these remarks. He made this statement: "People who are in good health do not need a doctor. Sick people do. Go and learn the meaning of the words: 'It is mercy I desire and not sacrifice!'"

Sacrifice refers to the ritual oblations prescribed by the Law through which one hoped to atone for one's sins. But it is mercy that God is most interested in, according to Jesus, not rituals. He does not mean to infer that sacred rites have no value at all, but to use them as a standard to judge other people is not the right use of them. We never know as we look at certain people, and wonder about how they are earning a living, whether in a few seconds they may be completely changed.

When Jesus said, "I've come to call not the self-righteous, but sinners," this was big news. This statement warns those who pursue the spiritual journey to be aware of the serious disease that afflicts them. Contemplative prayer is a kind of antibiotic for this disease. Notice the heavy irony in Jesus' words. "I have come to call not the self-righteous, but sinners." Everybody suffers from the disease of the human condition (original sin) and is therefore a sinner. It is just a matter of degree. People who think they are not sick, who regard themselves as righteous or God's greatest gifts to humanity, are the subject of Jesus' ironic statement: "People in good health do not need a doctor. Sick people do." To paraphrase: "If you are willing to recognize the disease of the false self, I am at your service."

This juxtaposition of people who know they are sinners and those who do not know they are sinners though they are just as sick occurs in the parables. Take the prodigal son. As soon as the profligate comes home, he is treated to a celebration rather like the celebration that Jesus attended for Matthew. The sacrament of reconciliation is not only the confession of sins, but the celebration that our sins have been forgiven. It is the same kind of event that the prodigal son celebrated and that Matthew is celebrating in this text. Self-righteous people can not understand how God can celebrate the return of profligates, crooks and extortionists just because they seem to have turned over a new leaf. The respectability that tends to cling to us when we lead a fairly good life hides our own tendency to prefer ourselves to the rights and needs of others.

When the prodigal son comes home, there is a celebration. Then we hear about the dutiful son who always stayed home. He turns out to be a bigger sinner than his brother. He judges him harshly and then refuses to celebrate his recovery. He complains bitterly that his father never gave him even a goat to celebrate with his friends. Notice the envy and jealousy that he manifests. This dutiful son, although to all appearances well behaved, was still unredeemed.

We too, like the elder son, may question why the prodigal was received with open arms and a celebration. The answer is because he needs it, not because he deserves it. The dutiful son is not able to understand the compassion of this father who obviously represents God. We do this all the time in our spiritual journey. If we are left unconsoled for awhile, or if a little too much truth about ourselves comes up too fast, we back away instead of plunging into the infinite mercy of God. Obvious sinners seem to be in a better situation. When they hit bottom, where else can they go except into the mercy of God? We could go there without having to hit bottom if we recognized that we too are sinners in need of healing.

FROM THE TEACHINGS
OF JESUS

17

WAITING FOR GOD

"Gird your loins and light your lamps and be like servants who await their master's return from a wedding, ready to open immediately when he comes and knocks. Blessed are those servants whom the master finds vigilant on his arrival. Amen, I say to you, he will gird himself, have them recline at table, and proceed to wait on them. And should he come in the second or third watch and find them prepared in this way, blessed are those servants. Be sure of this: if the master of the house had known the hour when the thief was coming, he would not have let his house be broken into. You also must be prepared, for at an hour you do not expect, the Son of Man will come."

(Luke 12:35–40)

Abraham did not know where he was going when he was called by the Lord. He is the paradigm of faith, especially contemplative faith that is willing to follow God's call into the unknown without knowing where it is going. In fact, that is the only way to go. As soon as we think we know where we are going, we are on the wrong road.

The Lord offers two parables in this text, both of which deal with the lack of certitude. In the first, the servant does not know when the master is coming back from the wedding. The second

69

parable states that if the head of the house knew when the thief was coming, he would stay awake. These parables reinforce the idea that the spiritual journey is not programmed and cannot be computerized. You have to be willing to put up with the uncertainty, which means waiting, being on guard, and doing your job while you wait. These parables are ways of inveighing against our inveterate demand to know where we are going, what is going to happen, what the end of the journey is and if possible, the exact date on which transforming union will transpire.

Let us see if we can catch the twinkle in Jesus' eyes as he addresses these parables to his students. He says, "Let your belts be fastened around your waist and your lamps burning brightly and be like servants awaiting the master's return from a wedding." This teaching is about how we are to feel as we wait upon God in prayer. Jesus says, "Think of me as being at a wedding." He wants us to presume that he has a good reason for delaying his appearance and asks that we not indulge in complaints or hold his absence against him. The purpose of waiting is to be ready when he finally arrives so that we can open to him without delay and enjoy his presence.

Jesus goes on to say, "It will go well with those servants whom the master finds wide awake. I tell you he will put on an apron, seat them at table and proceed to wait on them." To paraphrase, "Friends, if you don't complain because I lingered so long at the party, you won't believe the service I will give you. I may come at midnight or just before the dawn. If you can hang on till then, you will see me emerging out of the darkness."

The Lord knows perfectly well that we, like the disciples at Lake Tiberias, have worked hard and caught nothing, and that all our efforts have been fruitless. Still we wait. When the dawn begins to show, the peace of Christ silently steals into our inmost being and overflows into all the senses.

Now Jesus shifts the image. Again notice the humor. "You know that if the head of the house knew when the thief was coming, he would not let him break into his house." Jesus represents himself as an unexpected intruder. This parable refers not just to physical death, but to all his unexpected intrusions into our lives that take us by surprise. Sometimes he comes when we are at our lowest ebb. All of a sudden, in the midst of anguish, anger, bitterness, lustful thoughts, and the feeling of abandonment, this incredibly loving presence appears as if to say, "Well, what is the matter with you? What are you belly-aching about? Because it got a little dark, you didn't see me. Be on guard, therefore, because the son of man will come when you least expect him."

When we least expect him is the darkest part of the night. It is not our pleas that bring the master back; he comes when he sees that we have completed our preparation. The pain of waiting is in proportion to the joy of resurrection. To those on the spiritual journey nothing happens that is not directed toward divine union if they only say "Yes."

If we can't say "Yes," we should just wait and not say anything. Then at least we won't say "No."

18

FORGIVENESS

Then Peter approaching asked him, "Lord, if my brother sins against me, how often must I forgive him? As many as seven times?" Jesus answered, "I say to you, not seven times but seventy-seven times. That is why the kingdom of heaven may be likened to a king who decided to settle accounts with his servants. When he began the accounting, a debtor was brought before him who owed him a huge amount. Since he had no way of paying it back, his master ordered him to be sold, along with his wife, his children, and all his property, in payment of the debt. At that, the servant fell down, did him homage, and said, 'Be patient with me and I will pay you back in full.' Moved with compassion, the master of that servant let him go and forgave him the loan. When that servant had left, he found one of his fellow servants who owed him a much smaller amount. He seized him and started to choke him, demanding, 'Pay back what you owe.' Falling to his knees, his fellow servant begged him, 'Be patient with me, and I will pay you back.' But he refused. Instead, he had him put in prison until he paid back the debt. Now when his fellow servants saw what had happened, they were deeply disturbed, and went to their master and reported the whole affair. His master summoned him and said to him,

*'You wicked servant! I forgave you your entire debt because
you begged me to. Should you not have had pity on your fellow servant, as I had pity on you?' Then in anger his master
handed him over to the torturers until he should pay back
the whole debt.*

*So will my heavenly Father do to you, unless each of you
forgives his brothers and sisters from the heart."*

(Matt. 18:21–35)

All of the Lord's parables tend to upset the approved or
accepted value systems of his time. The Old Testament urged
people to forgive their fellow citizens. But it was a bit much to
expect people to forgive foreigners. The idea of forgiveness was
pushed far beyond any limitation by the example and teaching
of Jesus. He makes it clear that whatever may have been the ac-
ceptable teaching up to that time, he was now proposing a new
teaching, namely, that one is to forgive again and again without
any limitation.

This teaching came as a surprise to Peter and the other disciples trained in the religious milieu of their time. Peter thought
that he was being very generous in proposing to forgive offenses
up to seven times. He was expecting a pat on the back when he
came up with this formula. As often happened, Peter miscalcu-
lated and was reproved. Jesus said, "You must forgive not just
seven times but seventy times seven." Since seven is a perfect
number, the clear implication is that complete forgiveness is the
meaning of the Law.

The parable describes what happened to someone in heavy
debt who was about to be put in jail. He prostrates in front of
the king to whom he owes a huge sum and pleads for mercy.
The king forgave the whole debt. This was a marvelous act of
generosity for those days.

The debtor, now freed from the debt he could not pay, barely
got out the door when he met one of his own debtors who owed
him a small sum. He grabs the man by the throat and says, "Give

me my money or else!" The debtor falls on his face pleading, "Give me time and I will pay you all."

But the first debtor would not listen and had him put in jail along with his wife and children.

The servants were upset and reported the whole thing to the king. He was furious. Isn't that the way you would feel? Yet the forgiveness of debts was not part of the mentality of the time. The debtor who was forgiven was so attached to the expectation of getting his money that he could not change his way of acting. The king in anger handed him over to the torturers. The punch line is: "My heavenly father will treat you in the same way if you do not forgive your brothers and sisters from your heart."

The teaching being presented has a certain vigor. Jesus tells Peter, "Not only should you forgive your brother seven times, but any number of times." This is a new way of thinking about forgiveness. Human beings have felt from time immemorial that if they are offended, they are entitled to revenge. Revenge resists the open-heartedness to which the gospel calls us. Jesus, in these harsh terms, manifests the maternal character of God. We live in a patriarchal culture. This is not the same as a paternal culture; a patriarchal culture is one in which domination is emphasized rather than the nurturing and concern that goes with a true father.

Forgiveness represents the tender side of God. Tenderness is normally associated with feminine sensitivity. God claims the feminine character for himself in a number of places in Scripture as for instance in Isaiah, "Even if a mother forgets the child of her womb, I will not forget you."

The universe is the womb of God out of which every creature emerges. What is the essential aspect of a womb? It is the life giving milieu in which the bond between the child and its mother develops. This bond must be continued outside the womb if the child is to grow into a normal human being. In this parable, the importance of forgiveness as the essential healing of a bond that has been injured emerges in full force. The health and integrity of every community, its creativity and growth, depends on the sense of belonging. Forgiveness is a necessity from this perspective; it is the very fabric of the universe.

The outstretched arms of Jesus on the cross are the symbol of the forgiveness of everything and everyone. This love triumphs over the forces of entropy in creation. In a sense, unwillingness to forgive is an attack upon God. God is so identified with creation that any unwillingness to forgive is a resistance to grace; any movement to injure another is to tear God to pieces.

The bond of love needs to be constantly renewed. Forgiveness maintains and strengthens the bond of unity that enables all life to grow. If we have much to forgive, we also have much to be forgiven. The proportion between the two, the parable suggests, is very small.

19

THE DUTY OF CONFRONTATION

"If your brother sins [against you], go and tell him his fault between you and him alone. If he listens to you, you have won over your brother. If he does not listen, take one or two others along with you, so that 'every fact may be established on the testimony of two or three witnesses.' If he refuses to listen to them, tell the church. If he refuses to listen even to the church, then treat him as you would a Gentile or a tax collector. Amen, I say to you, whatever you bind on earth shall be bound in heaven, and whatever you loose on earth shall be loosed in heaven. Again, [amen,] I say to you, if two of you agree on earth about anything for which they are to pray, it shall be granted to them by my heavenly Father. For where two or three are gathered together in my name, there am I in the midst of them."

(Matt. 18:15–20)

The duty of confrontation is a hard one. According to this text, if you see people doing something seriously wrong, there is an obligation, given certain norms of prudence, to bring this fault to their attention so that they do not disintegrate into more and more self-destructive behavior. Just how far this applies to us depends on our vocation. There seems to be a prophetic role in which one is sent by God to call leaders or other people to

76

order. There have been some classical examples in history of people who under the inspiration of the Spirit confronted highly placed people with their faults. We only have to think of John the Baptist who lost his head or Thomas More who complained about the conduct of Henry VIII in similar circumstances and also found himself headless. Certain hazards surround the prophetic role. Hence it is just as well to make sure that we are really sent before we confront the lions in their dens. All of us, however, have to face the duty to correct someone once in a while.

Dealing with teenagers is a constant concern for parents. There is anxiety over whether children are getting into bad company, experimenting with drugs, or exploring conduct that is not suitable for teenagers. At a certain point you may have enough indication of trouble to say, "I must confront this child." At the same time, you want to be sure that whatever correction you offer comes out of genuine concern and love.

Confrontation never works if it comes out of a feeling of anger. Hence, it is important to choose a suitable time and place and to consider what the other person's situation is so that you have the maximum chance of speaking to their heart.

Some people are temperamentally inclined to confront people; nothing gives them greater pleasure. If our correction comes from the enjoyment of confrontation, it is not going to get anywhere. Others cannot bring themselves to confront anyone because of shyness or timidity which does not want to rock the boat and inclines them to sweep all kinds of garbage under the rug. Eventually there is no more space under the rug; the dirt comes out anyway and makes a terrible mess. If they had confronted the problem promptly and out of love, they might have done a great service to someone they love or whom they have a responsibility to correct.

The Lord indicates that if you have tried to correct and have not succeeded, you have fulfilled your duty and no more is expected of you other than to go on praying. He suggests a way of handling difficulties in a community when things are not going well with some of the members: pull them aside and confront them. This is called fraternal correction. If that does not work, you bring in a few prudent persons to discuss the matter; and if that does not work, you bring in the community as a whole. If all these efforts fail, you have completed your duty and now you can treat the offender like tax collectors whom everybody avoids. You still love the person, but the duty of trying to correct him or her has gone as far as it can go.

Love alone can change people. This is the great confrontation that no one can resist. It offers others space in which to change no matter what they do. Our ill-conceived efforts, especially if they arise from personal annoyance or because the conduct of others might cause us embarrassment, will accomplish nothing. The offenders will sense that the confrontation is not coming from a genuine concern for them and will mobilize their defenses. By showing love no matter what happens we provide them with a milieu in which they can experience the possibility of changing. This is to imitate God's compassion toward us. He is constantly trying to correct us but never with vindictiveness. When he corrects us, he never pursues us like the three Furies of Greek mythology. He simply keeps inviting us to let go of conduct that is self-destructive and to come back to his love. Whenever there is something to be corrected, he indicates that if we amend, we will enjoy complete forgiveness. The only confrontation that leads to correction is to accept whomever we are trying to help just as they are.

Here is a true story about a psychiatric nurse who was told the lurid history of a certain patient who had just entered the hospital. This man had committed a terrible crime. It was so terrible that he never wanted it known. He had completed his long prison sentence and had come to the hospital in a dying condition. He could not believe that God could forgive his crime;

hence, he resisted any form of reconciliation. The chaplain tried to persuade him to trust God. He refused. Any thought of reconciliation awakened his self-hatred. It was more painful for him to think of forgiveness than to feel his self-hatred.

The psychiatric nurse showed him every courtesy. She tucked him in at night, provided him with little favors like flowers, remembered his birthday, asked about his family, and wrote him notes on her day off. Because his illness was prolonged, she developed a friendship with him.

Near the end, his closest friend came to see him and urged him to be reconciled with God. "Please don't mention it!" the dying man pleaded. "God couldn't possibly forgive me for what I have done."

His friend kept urging, "God is good! He loves you. You can trust him." But nothing he said could penetrate the sick man's defenses.

Finally the friend said in desperation, "Think how much love the nurse shows you. Couldn't God do the same?" The sick man acknowledged how grateful he was to the nurse who had shown him so much love, but he added, "If she knew what I have done, she too would reject me."

His friend replied, "I must make a confession to you. When you first entered the hospital, I confided to her the entire story of your crime in every detail." The dying man looked at him in stunned astonishment. His defenses dissolved and his eyes filled with tears. "If she could love me," he murmured, "knowing all that I have done, it must be true. God too can love me."

This nurse ministered the sacrament of reconciliation not ritually but actually. She communicated in her very person God's forgiveness and compassion. The sacrament of reconciliation was unacceptable to him, but God came to him in a person who was able to manifest God's love for him in a concrete way. This is the ultimate confrontation which is not so much a confrontation as the transmission of divine love. The Ultimate Reality, whom Jesus called Abba, is the loving father, mother and every human relationship that is beautiful, good, and true all rolled into one transcendent gift of boundless compassion. Each of us can be a symbol of that love to those we meet.

20

FREEDOM FROM CULTURAL CONDITIONING

Great crowds were traveling with him, and he turned and addressed them, "If anyone comes to me without hating his father and mother, wife and children, brothers and sisters, and even his own life, he cannot be my disciple. Whosoever does not carry his own cross and come after me, cannot be my disciple. Which of you wishing to construct a tower does not first sit down and calculate the cost to see if there is enough for its completion? Otherwise, after laying the foundation and finding himself unable to finish the work the onlookers should laugh at him and say, 'This one began to build but did not have the resources to finish.' Or what king marching into battle would not first sit down and decide whether with ten thousand troops he can successfully oppose another king advancing upon him with twenty thousand troops? But if not, while he is still far away, he will send a delegation to ask for peace terms. In the same way, everyone of you who does not renounce all his possessions cannot be my disciple."

(Luke 14:25-33)

The text presents Jesus on his way along a road accompanied by a huge crowd. I suppose it occurred to him to ask, who

81

are these people who are following me and what is their motivation? In any case, he turned around and presented them with
the wisdom saying recorded in this text, which I paraphrase:
"Unless you who are following me are prepared to hate your
mother, father, wife, children, brothers and sisters, you might as
well go home. Unless you are ready to turn your backs on the
people who are closest to you, you cannot be my follower." Then
he added, "You also have to hate your own life, your very self,
your own thoughts, judgments, hang-ups." This is a big order.
Since quite a few continued to follow him, he proceeded to add
two parables by way of clarification.

Before building a house, a prudent person draws up a blue-
print and, depending on the height of the building, plans the
foundation accordingly. Jesus commented: "Reflect on what being a follower of mine is. Don't just follow me blindly. What is
it going to cost you? Think of the foundation required for this
building and to what you are committing yourself."

The sayings of Jesus are designed to move people to question
their unquestioned values so that they can be open to the radical
program for change that he offers. We do not normally enjoy
change; even a change for the better is threatening. It is easier
to stick with the value system that we have absorbed from our
parents, education, ethnic group, nation and religious education.
Jesus regularly invited his hearers to question their value system.
In the culture of his time, family was the supreme value. Today
when the family is breaking up in the Western world, Jesus might
have said the reverse. Again, the tendency nowadays is not to
take proper care of the old folks; they are an embarrassment and
a burden. So in our time we need to hear just the opposite of
this saying. The point is that Jesus' wisdom sayings challenge
our unquestioned values in whatever age we live.

One well-known person who carried out this wisdom saying
was Francis of Assisi. He came from a fine home; his father was a
successful businessman and highly respected in the community.
Like most parents, he thought it would be nice if his children

would marry someone chosen by their parents, have a good income, home, children, take care of them in their old age, bury them, and lovingly remember them. These were normal human expectations of the time. Unfortunately, they become institutionalized over a long period of time, and come to be considered as the supreme values. Then when anyone hesitated about any part of the expected scenario, the resistance of relatives and friends was enormous.

When we are called, as Jesus is implying, to a higher set of values that involves the service not just of our immediate family, but of a broader scope, as in the case of the apostles, then these unquestioned values stand in the way. Hence, Jesus warns, if the accepted values oppose or prevent us from growing beyond them, we must "hate" our cultural attachments and launch out into the unknown. We must be ready to renounce the values we have interiorized when these oppose the values of the Gospel.

When Francis left home and possessions, his father felt insulted, hurt and rejected. His plans for Francis were turned upside down. This seems to be a normal parental experience. Because it is so difficult to distinguish human loyalty from the higher loyalty of God's call, the agonizing moments of this period of our conversion requires us to sit down and figure out what this choice is going to cost. Then we will not be surprised when those we love accuse us of disregarding their love for us.

Francis succeeded in disidentifying himself from the limited values of his family and culture. He was like the past generation of hippies who rejected the material values of their parents. Unfortunately that generation transferred their dependency structures from the home to the commune or peer group and continued the same cycle of dependency. An institution can be helpful in gathering up this generosity and channeling it to good purposes. The struggle to let go of over-identification needs to be guided; there is a thin line between a true vocation and fanaticism in hanging on to a vision that is not sufficiently nuanced or in dialogue with other human values. The harsh sayings of

Jesus are balanced by instructions that seem to contradict them. For example, Jesus accused the Pharisees of avoiding the duty of the financial support of parents by promising their inheritance to the Temple, which was an evasion of the practical love owed to parents. These balancing statements warn us that what Jesus is teaching is the inward freedom from over-identification that prevents human growth. It is not a denial of what we owe in gratitude to our parents, but the freedom to go beyond their particular world-view.

21

THE NARROW DOOR

He passed through towns and villages, teaching as he went and making his way to Jerusalem. Someone asked him, "Lord, will only a few people be saved?" He answered them, "Strive to enter through the narrow gate, for many, I tell you, will attempt to enter but will not be strong enough. After the master of the house has arisen and locked the door, then will you stand outside knocking and saying, 'Lord, open the door for us.' He will say to you in reply, 'I do not know where you are from.' And you will say, 'We ate and drank in your company and you taught in our streets.' Then he will say to you, 'I do not know where [you] are from. Depart from me all you evildoers!'

"And there will be wailing and grinding of teeth when you see Abraham, Isaac, and Jacob and all the prophets in the kingdom of God and you yourselves cast out. And people will come from the east and the west, and from the north and the south and will recline at table in the kingdom of God. For behold, some are last who will be first, and some are first who will be last."

(Luke 13:22–30)

This was Jesus' last trip to Jerusalem, a trip which was to bring his life and teaching to a calamitous conclusion. In the forefront of Jesus' mind is the sacrifice of his life that he is about to offer for the redemption of the world. In the course of his teaching, someone asks, "Sir, are there going to be few or many saved?" Jesus, as a wisdom teacher, was well able to discern how serious this question was. Did this person really want to know the answer, or was this just a casual question prompted by curiosity?

This young man could be a genuine seeker passionately interested in the answer either for himself or for the sake of other people with whom he identifies. If you are engaged in the service of the retarded, the dying, the hungry, or the imprisoned, this is a crucial question. You really want to know. The question to which Jesus responds challenges us. Are there going to be few who are saved? If so, how do we become one of those few?

Notice how Jesus responds. He is on his way to his own death so he is not about to answer lightly. Are there few who are going to be saved? He does not answer the question directly. He simply enlarges the background and thus frees the questioner from a variety of limiting factors that would make it impossible for him to know the answer.

Jesus says first of all that one's external adherence to one's religion does not guarantee entrance into the kingdom of God. Those who think they are first will be last and those who are last will be first. Or again, people are going to come from the east, west, north, and south and take their places with the prophets while the insiders may find themselves outsiders. Thus, external adherence to the religion that embraces the revelation of God is not enough. A lot of people whom we do not expect to find in the kingdom are going to be there. Why? Because they have inwardly accepted the basic principle of the kingdom of God which is fidelity to one's conscience. Jesus does not indicate that those from the north, south, east, and west are going to be Christians. He just says that they are going to be there. How they got there is not addressed. He also says that those who think they are going to be there are not going to be there. In fact, when they bang on the door crying, "Lord, we heard you every Sunday in church, we ate and drank with you. You must know us," he will reply, "I never heard of you. Go away."

The external observances of religion by themselves are useless. Our actions must correspond with our beliefs. They are going to be the measure by which the master of the house, after he has gone to bed, will decide whether it is worth getting up to let us in.

These are the serious considerations that Jesus lays out for the reflection of this young man and for the broadening of his ideas. Already Jesus has delivered him from his over-identification with his cultural conditioning and religious self-image. Hence, the young man's question is put into a wholly new context.

Jesus replies, "Try to enter through the narrow gate." What is the narrow door that provides such great security? In a sheepfold the gate is extremely narrow. Only one sheep can go in or out at a time. Hence, there is an intimate relationship between the shepherd and the sheep. He calls each one by name.

The narrow door, in the context of Jesus' journey to Jerusalem and to his sacrificial death, is his teaching and example. It is not calling oneself a Christian but actually following Jesus that counts.

The basic teaching of Jesus is the unconditional acceptance of everyone. Although such a practice is extremely demanding, everyone has the capacity to do it because only two things are required — suffering and love. Everyone can suffer and everyone can love.

22

THE NEW WINE

Then the disciples of John approached him and said, "Why do we and the Pharisees fast [much] but your disciples do not fast?" Jesus answered them, "Can the wedding guests mourn as long as the bridegroom is with them? The days will come when the bridegroom is taken away from them, and then they will fast. No one patches an old cloak with a piece of unshrunken cloth, for its fullness pulls away from the cloak and the tear gets worse. People do not put new wine into old wineskins. Otherwise, the skins burst, the wine spills out, and the skins are ruined. Rather, they pour new wine into fresh wineskins, and both are preserved."

(Matt. 9:14–17)

John the Baptist made quite a stir in Israel and attracted many disciples. Jesus was baptized by him and drew his first disciples from among John's followers. John was austere. He wore a loincloth and ate only locusts and wild honey. He practiced much fasting and expected the same of his disciples.

When there are two spiritual teachers or religious communities in the same neighborhood, the loyalties of one group may conflict with the loyalties of the other. There may be some mutual denigrating and backbiting. Comparisons may be made between *our* observance and their observance, *our* spiritual teacher and their spiritual teacher, *our* tradition and their tradition.

In this incident, John's disciples were sniping at the disciples of Jesus. They said, "How is it that the Pharisees and we fast and you folks do not?" implying that Jesus' disciples were not measuring up to the high standards of John's. "Who are you," is the implication of the question, "compared with us?" An austere observance draws public attention, admiration, and acclaim.

Jesus graciously adjusts himself to these human foibles. He responds with a question of his own, "How can the wedding guests go mourning while the bridegroom is with them?" implying that John's disciples are not seeing the whole picture. They are looking for holiness, but in the wrong place. He adds, "When the bridegroom is taken away, then the wedding guests will fast."

He appeals to the fact that his presence among his disciples is a celebration and that it is not appropriate to mourn while attending a wedding. At the very least, they will not be welcome guests. A celebration requires the capacity to receive as well as to give in order to apply this insight into our personal experience of grace. When God graciously comes into our lives for a few minutes, it is not the time to practice our customary austerities. It is like having a surprise visit from a dear relative who comes to share affection and love, and who finds us too busy with various chores to say anything but, "Come back some other time."

Jesus continues, "Nobody sews a piece of unshrunken cloth on an old cloak. That will only make the rip bigger." And he adds, "People do not pour new wine into old wineskins." An old wineskin dries out, shrivels, and cracks. If we put new wine into it, the chemicals that are still being processed in the new wine will burst the old skin. The old skin does not have the flexibility to expand with the effervescence.

New wine is a marvelous image of the Holy Spirit. As we move to the intuitive level of consciousness through contemplative prayer, the energy of the Spirit cannot be contained in the old structures. They are not flexible enough. They may have to be left aside or adapted. The new wine as a symbol of the Spirit has a tendency to stir people up; for that reason, the Fathers of the Church called it "sober intoxication." Although its exuberance is subdued, it breaks out of categories and cannot be contained in neat boxes.

Jesus points out to John's disciples that they have a good practice but are too attached to fasting as a structure. The wine of the Spirit that Jesus brings will not fit into their narrow ideas. They must expand their views. Otherwise, the new wine of the gospel will give them trouble. It will burst the narrow confines of their mind sets, and both what they have and what they are trying to receive will be lost.

Jesus suggests a solution: "Put the new wine into new wineskins." The new wine of the Gospel is manifested by the fruits of the Spirit which are nine aspects of the mind of Christ. If the new wine is to be preserved, new structures have to be found that are more appropriate than the old ones. If we lean too heavily on the old structures, the new wine of the Spirit will be lost. This happened in the late Middle Ages and especially in the post-Reformation Church when the emphasis moved from cultivating the fruits of the Spirit to conformity to doctrinal formulas and external observances. That is why we found ourselves at the time of Vatican II in a spiritual desert. The old wine had run out. Renewal in the Spirit, the new wine, is our recovery of the contemplative tradition of Christianity. But this movement of the Spirit has to be put into new structures; the old ones are likely to burst.

Is it possible to renovate old wineskins? With a lot of greasing they may regain some flexibility, but not as much as new ones. The process may also take a long time.

What will happen with the renewal of contemplative life among the lay folks? We will see new forms of contemplative lifestyle that better serve the new wine with its tendency to expand, excite, and go to one's head, so to speak. The new wine is the contemplative dimension of the Gospel. Its basic act is consent to the presence and action of the Spirit within us. This consent is directed not to our intentionality but to God's intentionality. The Spirit who loved us first is pouring the wine, not we. It is a mistake to think that we have to win God's attention or impress him with our virtues. That is not the new wine. That is an attitude that belongs to the old wine where efforts are viewed as a necessary means of winning God's favor.

If we consent to God's intentionality, he works in us through the fruits of the Spirit: boundless compassion, joy, peace, and the others enumerated by Paul (Gal. 5:22–23). No structure can contain such wine. Paul adds, "Those who are moved by the Spirit have no Law." They are beyond any law because they fulfill the purpose of all laws, which is the continuous flow of divine love and compassion. Thus they fulfill every just law spontaneously.

CELEBRATIONS
OF JESUS' PRESENCE

23

CHRISTMAS

*Now there were shepherds in that region living in the fields
and keeping the night watch over their flock. The angel of
the Lord appeared to them and the glory of the Lord shone
around them, and they were struck with great fear. The angel
said to them, "Do not be afraid; for behold, I proclaim to
you good news of great joy that will be for all the people.
For today in the city of David a savior has been born for you
who is Messiah and Lord. And this will be a sign for you:
you will find an infant wrapped in swaddling clothes and
lying in a manger." And suddenly there was a multitude of
the heavenly host with the angel, praising God and saying:*

*"Glory to God in the highest
and on earth peace to those on whom his favor rests."*

(Luke 2:8–14)

All kinds of mysteries come spilling out of the Gospel on
Christmas, tumbling and cascading down to every level of our
consciousness. Let us join the shepherds and try to enter into
their experience. Events and images in Scripture symbolize inner
experiences. Christmas is, therefore, an important occasion in
our personal history. Through it God awakens us to the divine
life in us. We are not only human beings; we are divinely human

beings. The angels, by word and action, impressed upon the shepherds the meaning of the newborn child. The liturgy tries to do the same by word and sacrament.

It is important to realize that the Scriptures are based on a cosmology that taught that everything in creation could be reduced to four basic elements — earth, air, fire, and water. The sacraments of the Church have inherited this cultural mentality. In our collective unconscious these elements are still powerful, and they are always at work in us. What happened in the fields outside Bethlehem was that an angel of the Lord appeared with the brightness of fire. His appearance was frightening at first. But as he spoke to the shepherds and calmed their fear, the light that accompanied him was suddenly magnified thousands of times, and "the glory of God shone around them." The overload of their senses catapulted the shepherds into a dazzling interior illumination. Then, the angel gave them a sign as in the tradition of the great theophanies of the Old Testament: "You will find the infant in a manger, wrapped in swaddling clothes."

Suddenly his voice was magnified thousands of times as numberless angels appeared out of the stars, out of the clear night sky, out of the fields, and out of the ground — all singing, shouting, and glorifying God! This tremendous overload of their senses stunned the shepherds into an inner harmony and integration. They hastened to Bethlehem to see the promised sign. They found the Christ Child lying in a manger. Did they cradle him in their arms and through that touch grasp the presence of the Word within their hearts?

Elijah on Mount Horeb experienced an overload of his sense perceptions in the form of a raging fire, a whirlwind, and an earthquake. But it was only in the still small voice that he recognized the presence of God. His was one of the peak experiences of the Old Testament. But it was not the fullness of the Gospel. Something more has been given. Now God has become one of us and is breathing our air. In Jesus, God's heart is beating; his eyes are seeing; his hands are touching; his ears are hearing.

Through his humanity, the whole material universe has become divine. Now God is *in* the whirlwind, *in* the earthquake, and *in* the raging fire. By becoming a human being, he is in the heart of all creation and in every part of it.

On the Feast of Epiphany the liturgy celebrates this insight and sings of the waters of the Jordan sanctified by the touch of the body of Jesus. Every drop of water on earth, as a result of that contact, has become matter for the sacrament of baptism. It has become the material element for the transmission of divine life. Similarly, by eating and drinking, Jesus has made food and drink, especially bread and wine, the means of divine transformation.

The overload from some strong sense experience that speaks of God not only points to him, but in some mysterious way contains him. Now Jesus can say that whatever is done to the least of his little ones is done to him. Every human person, by virtue of the Incarnation, is Christ.

Everything in creation has been transformed by contact with his humanity. By his breathing, the atmosphere is sacred. By his eating, food is sacred. Now every sense experience conveys the mystery of Christ. "The Word was made flesh" — made a part of creation, made matter — "and dwells among us." Jesus gives himself to us in everything that happens.

24

EPIPHANY

When you read this you can understand my insight into the mystery of Christ, which was not made known to human beings in other generations as it has now been revealed to his holy apostles and prophets by the Spirit, that the Gentiles are coheirs, members of the same body, and copartners in the promise in Christ Jesus through the gospel.

(Eph. 3:4–6)

This feast is a study of the manifestations of Christ in his divine nature. It is clear from the readings for this day that the liturgy has three important epiphanies in mind. In each of these appearances Christ manifested his divine nature in and through his humanity.

Somehow the divinity of the child was manifested to the Magi. Somehow the divine nature of Christ was manifested to John the Baptist and his disciples at the river bank of the Jordan. Somehow his divine nature was manifested to his disciples when he changed water into wine at the marriage feast of Cana. What is the significance of these divine manifestations the liturgy has picked out to celebrate on the Feast of the Epiphany? It is obvious that the Church is hoping that in the course of the celebration of this Christmas-Epiphany cycle we too will be awakened to the same perception of the divinity of Jesus. How that will happen, when it will happen, how profoundly it will happen — this is all part of the mystery. But it *is* happening.

The grace of Epiphany is the call to become divine. Christ's birth as man is nothing less than the visible expression of his eternal birth as the Word of God in the eternal silence of the Father. Of course, in the Father, silence is the fullness of everything. This silence — fullness becoming aware of itself — is the Word, God's Son. Epiphany is the celebration of the grace of this eternal birth in us. This is effected, after the pattern of our Lady, by our informed consent.

The substance of the question that the angel Gabriel put to Mary was: "Are you willing to become the mother of God's Son?"

How could she be the mother of God's Son without in some way becoming divine herself? Thus, the real question the angel asked was: "Mary, will you consent to become divine?"

A second question seems to be implied: "Will you consent to manifest God in your body?"

You would think that anyone would jump at the chance of becoming divine while still in this life. But we are scared to death of such a prospect. Even Mary and Joseph, the two who were best prepared, hesitated to become involved in the mystery of the Incarnation. Although there is something in every human being that reaches out for unlimited life and happiness by becoming one with God, there is also something in us that is afraid of being squashed by his transcendence. Of course, God is infinitesimal as well as infinite, gentle as well as powerful. There is no danger of his stepping on us. Like the hart leaping over the mountains in the Song of Solomon, he is more surefooted than any creature.

Our Lady is the heart of the human response to God because her consent is the source of everyone's consent. We will never consent to God as fully as we can until we understand what her consent really meant. She gave the most practical advice of all time in her offhand remark to the waiters at the marriage feast of Cana. "Do," she said, "whatever he tells you." That is precisely what she did. To do the will of another is, in a sense, to become the other. To do God's will is to lose one's own separate identity. To consent to the fact of God's interior presence is to know where you came from and where you are going. It is to know who you are.

"Do you consent to become divine?" That is the question asked of us today.

The second question is more concrete. "Will you consent to express me, your God, in your body?" That is scary! To be God in everything we say and do and are! Such is the radical consent that our Lady gave. The Church, in her irrepressible ambition for each of us, invites us to do the same.

25

THE FEAST OF SAINT JOSEPH

Now this is how the birth of Jesus Christ came about. When his mother Mary was betrothed to Joseph, but before they lived together, she was found with child through the holy Spirit. Joseph her husband, since he was a righteous man, yet unwilling to expose her to shame, decided to divorce her quietly.

(Matt. 1:18–19)

Just as Abraham became the father of all who have faith by renouncing the possibility of an heir, so Joseph became the husband of Mary only after he had given up his plan to marry her. This is all about the loss and finding of Mary. It parallels the loss and finding of Jesus in the Temple. Joseph had set his heart on living with Mary as his wife. When her mysterious pregnancy broke up his plan, he decided that he had to give up the vision he had formed for his life — his plan of serving God with Mary as his wife. Can you think of anybody harder to give up than our Blessed Mother? The cause of his broken heart was Jesus himself. That is a significant pattern in the Christian life. Later Joseph had to go through the loss and finding of Jesus in the Temple, an even deeper participation in the mystery of Christ's passion, death and resurrection.

Every true seeker of God, from the beginning of time to the end of the world, has to pass through this mysterious inward death and rebirth, perhaps many times over. Joseph's love of Mary and his vision of life with her — and later his love of Jesus and his vision of life with him — were his two great visions, both given to him by God and both seemingly taken away from him by circumstances God arranged. These were the two eyes that he had to give up in order to see with God's eyes. He had to surrender his personal vision in order to become *Vision itself.* That, after all, is the goal and term of Christian life.

God grant us people with great vision! By that I mean men and women who dedicate themselves to some great ideal or purpose. Vision is what gives ordinary life its direction and invests it with purpose. As one journeys across the desert, prairie, or sea — all images of ordinary life in spiritual literature — one may come upon various places of rest: an oasis, a garden of spiritual delights, or a harbor. This can be an occasion of terrible temptation for a person with great vision. One seems to have arrived at the end of one's laborious journey and all one's immense efforts seem to be coming to fruition. Actually, the place of rest will become a place of poison unless one hastens to push on. Spiritual consolation is enervating when sought for its own sake.

But how does one push on? Is it by giving up the vision? Not exactly. Rather, it is by being *willing* to do so. For that ultimate renunciation is the only way to move beyond what one *thinks* is the vision and to embrace what it really *is.* In other words, it is necessary to give up all one's own ideas of how to reach the place of vision in order to get there. Thus, Abraham was told by God, at the most critical moment of his life, "Take your son...Isaac, whom you love, and go to the land of Moriah, and offer him there as a burnt offering upon one of the mountains of which I shall tell you" (Gen. 22:2). To paraphrase the text: "Take your great vision, your ideal of the spiritual journey and how to attain it, and go to the place I will show you. There sacrifice it to me."

The struggle to attain to the "land of vision," if one does not settle for something less along the way, leads to disappointment or even to what is close to despair. It is like dying. Your world must be broken! And you with it! Your idea of vocation, of the spiritual journey, of the church, of Jesus Christ, even of God himself, must be *shattered*. The crux of the human predicament that Jesus took upon himself does not consist simply of our personal sins. It is our sinful condition — all that causes us merely to reflect about the vision rather than *experience* it.

26

PASSION SUNDAY

When they drew near Jerusalem and came to Bethphage on the Mount of Olives, Jesus sent two disciples, saying to them, "Go into the village opposite you, and immediately you will find an ass tethered, and a colt with her. Untie them and bring them here to me. And if anyone should say anything to you, reply, 'The master has need of them.' Then he will send them at once." This happened so that what had been spoken through the prophet might be fulfilled:

> *"Say to daughter Zion,*
> *'Behold, your king comes to you,*
> *meek and riding on an ass,*
> *and on a colt,*
> *the foal of a beast of burden.' "*

The disciples went and did as Jesus had ordered them. They brought the ass and the colt and laid their cloaks over them. The very large crowd spread their cloaks on the road, while others cut branches from the trees and strewed them on the road. The crowds preceding him and those following kept crying out and saying:

> *"Hosanna to the Son of David;*
> *blessed is he who comes in the name of the Lord;*
> *hosanna in the highest."*

*And when he entered Jerusalem the whole city was shaken
and asked, "Who is this?" And the crowds replied, "This is
Jesus the prophet, from Nazareth in Galilee."*

(Matt. 21:1–11)

*Some of the Pharisees in the crowd said to him, "Teacher,
rebuke your disciples." He said in reply, "I tell you, if they
keep silent, the stones will cry out!"*

(Luke 19:39–40)

This event constitutes the one earthly triumph of Jesus' life
and ministry. The crowd was following him because of the great
miracle he had wrought in raising Lazarus from the dead. The
sisters from Bethany and Lazarus were apparently well known.
As the crowd grew in numbers, Jesus sensed that the Father
was asking him to acquiesce to this acclamation. He sent ahead
for a beast of burden. For the first time, as far as we know,
he mounted. He was thus slightly above the crowd so that all
could see him. The people started pulling down branches from
the trees and throwing them in front of him. Their enthusiasm
became contagious. The whole city was plunged into excitement.
The crowd was waving palms, singing and proclaiming him to be
the son of David, the king of Israel of times past and the father
of the Messiah. The words clearly implied a divine visitation.
That is why the Pharisees demanded, "Stop your disciples from
crying out. They are making you equal to God." He replied, "If
they are quiet, the stones will cry out." All creation was bearing
witness to the coming to final term of the life of him who is the
source of all that is.

The thunderous shouts and applause of the immense crowd
form the background for Jesus' amazing entry into Jerusalem.
When he came to the brow of the Mount of Olives, the procession stopped and Jesus wept over Jerusalem. He wept because
the city could not perceive the great opportunity that it was
about to lose. He was fully aware that the authorities were plot-

ting his death and that the adulation he was receiving would soon turn to condemnation. The superficial enthusiasm of the crowd had a hollow ring.

Nothing could be worse public relations than to have the celebrity of the moment burst into tears, especially when you are trying to turn him into a king or a god. Jesus wept because of the deep tragedy that only he had eyes to perceive. "Jerusalem," he sobbed, "if only you had known the time of your visitation. Now it is too late." Thus, the city that he loved so much was fated to undergo total destruction. It did not know the time of its divine visitation.

Jesus is the paradigm of humanity, the universal human being, God's idea of human nature with its enormous potentialities. According to the great hymn of Paul to God's humility, the divine Person of the Word, source of everything that exists, did not cling to his divine dignity or prerogatives, but threw them all away. In God there seems to be the need not to be God. In creating, God, in a sense, dies, because he is no longer alone; he is completely involved in the evolution of these creatures whom he has made so lovable.

Christ emptied himself of the divine power that could have protected him and opened himself in total vulnerability as he stretched out his arms on the cross to embrace all human suffering. In the most real sense, we too are the body of God; we too are a new humanity in which the Word becomes flesh; we too can put ourselves in the service of the divine Word. Then God is experiencing human life through our senses, our emotions, and our thoughts. Each of us can give the eternal Word a new way in which he discovers his own infinite potentiality. Thus, God knows himself in us and experiences the human condition in all its ramifications. The Word lives in us, or more exactly, lives us. We are incorporated into the new creation that Christ has brought into the world by becoming a human being. We leave behind the false self and solidarity with Adam, which is solidarity in sin, death, and human misery. Jesus invites us to experience his consciousness of the Father, the Abba of infinite concern, the God who transcends both suffering and joy and manifests equally in both.

Christ on the donkey, waving aside the cheers of the crowd, is riding to his death. This is his way of revealing the heart of God once and for all in such a way that no one can ever doubt God's infinite mercy. The priest says over the bread and wine, "This is my Body." The power of those words extends to each of us as Christ awakens and celebrates his great sacrifice in our own hearts saying, "*You* are my body. *You* are my blood." You, with all of humanity, are a manifestation in the flesh of the new creation.

27

HOLY THURSDAY

Then [Jesus] poured water into a basin and began to wash the disciples' feet and dry them with the towel around his waist.

(John 13:5)

The texts read in the liturgy during Lent provide us with the means to understand the sacred mysteries of Holy Week. We think of the penitent woman who washed our Lord's feet with her tears and of Mary of Bethany who anointed his feet with the perfumed oil. It was the custom of the time to wash the feet of a guest, to offer him a kiss of welcome, and to anoint his head with ointment. It was not the custom, however, to kiss those feet or to wash them with one's tears; nor to place precious ointment of great price on the guest's feet rather than upon his head. Why such extremes on the part of these two devoted women?

They evidently wished to show that he was no ordinary guest. Surely the divine goodness, which praised the extravagance of these two women, would not do less than offer you and me the ordinary courtesies, if he invites us to his banquet table.

With this background in mind, we can understand why Jesus washed the feet of his disciples. They were to be his guests at the first eucharistic supper, just as we are his guests at the commemoration of it. This sharing in the body and blood of the god-Man is the pledge of a still greater banquet: the eating and drinking of immortal life and love at the eternal banquet of heaven, where our nourishment will be the divine essence itself.

But as guests at the banquet table of the Lord in this world, and as recipients of the divine hospitality, the disciples had to receive at least the ordinary marks of courtesy; that is, the washing of the feet, the kiss of welcome, and the anointing with oil. These three acts form an organic whole. Omitting any one of them would have been to fail in courtesy, something the Father would never do to guests invited to his supper. These three marks of courtesy correspond to the three stages of Christian initiation.

First comes the washing of the feet, symbol of baptism, which must precede the Eucharist. The Eucharist represents the kiss of welcome, the intimacy of union, and the mutual sharing of deep love. The anointing of the head with perfumed oil suggests the grace of the sacrament of confirmation. Jesus did not anoint the heads of his disciples on this occasion because the Spirit had not yet been poured out. After his passion and resurrection, however, this crowning courtesy was bestowed.

In our case, however, it is being bestowed in each reception of the Eucharist, especially in the yearly renewal of the Paschal mystery. We have seen John resting in Jesus' bosom at the Last Supper, a symbol foreshadowing and anticipating this grace. The anointing of Jesus by Mary of Bethany pointed to the outpouring of the Spirit upon him and upon all his members, especially those taking part in the supper. But John was given the reality beyond the symbol. Resting in Jesus' bosom, John received the grace of which the anointing of the head with ointment is the external sign.

These reminders of the divine hospitality, of the inconceivable courtesy that God has extended to us, make us approach the Paschal mystery with humble and grateful hearts. How can we thank the Lord for his invitation, for the incredible depth of his sharing?

Having purified our hearts by stirring up the grace of our baptism and looking forward to the fullness of the Spirit that we hope to receive, we consume the flesh of Christ which, like a live coal, bears within itself the eternal flame of the Spirit. As we receive Jesus into our hearts, our inmost being is set afire, and we are turned in the direction of the deepest reality of human life, the presence of the Trinity in the depths of our spirit.

28

THE PASCHAL VIGIL

Alleluia! Alleluia! Alleluia!
(Responsorial Psalm of the Easter Vigil)

When you hear the triple *Alleluia* that introduces the Easter season in a burst of joy, what do you hear? What happens inside of you when you hear those thrilling acclamations?

Do you only hear the sound *Alleluia* and think, how beautiful? Or do you say to yourself, "That poor man who is trying to sing! Why doesn't he get some instruction?" You might be right, but if that is your only reaction, you may miss the special grace of the occasion.

Perhaps your thoughts revolve around the meaning of the word *Alleluia*, recalling that it means something like *hurrah* — a cry of victory — and you reflect, "This is Easter! I must rejoice!" Perhaps some of you perceive a spontaneous joy at the thought of Christ's triumph over death; a peaceful sense of gratitude to God for his goodness; or a sense of how much he loves you, or how much you love him.

You may even experience something like a volcano exploding inside you — a tremendous burst of joyful energy coming from the deepest place inside of you, which causes you to forget all your own thoughts, the fatigue of the evening of the Paschal Vigil, and what happens afterward.

If you have such an experience, you are well prepared to celebrate the Paschal mystery. You touch the reality about which all the symbols of this night's liturgy are stammering. You penetrate the mystery of the resurrection of Christ. You identify with Christ when you forget yourself and are filled with his joy.

Did Jesus experience something similar when the Holy Spirit reached into the tomb, laid hold of his mortal body, lifted it up, and divinized it? Did he think, "I am rising from the dead" or "I am alive"? Or was it just the experience of life — beyond words, thoughts, or feelings? Sheer experience! Sheer joy! Sheer life!

Anyone who responds to the sound of the *Alleluia* with the sheer experience of oneness with Christ has understood the resurrection. Those who have not yet experienced this union should have no doubt, no hesitation, that God is calling them to this experience. He is calling us, especially through this liturgical celebration of his resurrection, to become what baptism has already made us. Baptism has been *done* to us. We did nothing to bring it about — even if we were baptized as adults. It is the sheer gift of God. Eternal life has begun in us. We are the sons of God, incorporated into Christ's body. His Spirit dwells in us. All our sins are forgiven. The darkness of our ignorance and the weakness of our will are being healed. And if anything is lacking to us, Christ, who is interceding for us in heaven at the right hand of the Father, will give us that too.

We were responding to this intuition if, at the moment we heard the *Alleluia*, we identified with Christ. He is ours by baptism. It only remains for us to become what we are and to enjoy what we possess.

The power of this holy night dispels all evil, washes guilt away, restores lost innocence....
                              (Easter Proclamation [Exultet]*)*

The liturgy of the Easter Vigil awakens us to the realization of Christ risen in our hearts by means of a marvelous array of images, words, and symbols. The magnificent hymn in honor of the Paschal candle, known as the *Exultet*, explains what is happening within us by means of these symbolic rites. This sacred vigil is itself the principal symbol, as it brings to mind the whole of salvation history, especially the passage of the people of Israel through the Red Sea, which we read about in the second lesson. The liturgy of this night is trying to prepare us for baptism or for the renewal of baptism and, in order to understand what that grace means, calls upon the whole of sacred history. The saving power of God is vigorously at work in baptism just as it was in the passage of the Israelites through the Red Sea, and just as it is in our passage tonight from darkness into light.

There are two principal moments in these sacred rites that we must grasp in order to enter deeply into the renewal of our baptismal vows. First of all, a quick flashback to what happens earlier on this evening. In the blessing of the new fire we pray, "O God, bless this new fire to dispel the darkness of our hearts and minds. Lead us by this light as you led Moses and his people through the Red Sea. Kindle in us the fire of your glory."

The new fire is the symbol of the power of the Holy Spirit leaping up from the ground on which Christ's blood was poured out. A flame is taken from the fire to light the Paschal candle and we pray again: "May the light of the Risen Christ dispel the darkness of our minds and hearts!" In the joining of flame to candlewick, we celebrate the moment in which Christ's spirit reentered his body and he rose in glory from the dead. Thus, the Paschal candle is clearly identified as the risen Christ in our midst. This symbol communicates what we celebrate on this night — the mystery that takes place inwardly beyond symbols and to which all the symbols and words are designed to lead us.

Recall what happens next. Having identified Christ as the pillar of fire that led the Israelites on their journey, we too pass through the Red Sea, symbolized by the procession through the long corridor in total darkness. That procession is for each of us a new salvific event. Just as the Egyptians, symbol of the tyranny of sin, were utterly destroyed when they tried to pursue the fleeing Israelites into the Red Sea, so our sin and guilt are destroyed once again and more profoundly than ever.

There are many dark nights. The way to distinguish the darkness of sin from the divine darkness is faith in the risen Christ. As we enter the church and other candles are lighted from the flame of the Paschal candle, the light begins to spread and illumine the darkness not by becoming brighter, but by communicating its own light. As each of us receives the flame, the light spreads until this whole building and everyone in it are illuminated. The lighted candle we hold in our hands is the symbol of what happens to us interiorly. Christ rises in our hearts — and we *perceive* it! It is not a question of emotion, but *conviction!* Christ destroys our sinfulness and brings us, through the procession in the darkened corridor, to a new level of innocence and to a new level of participation in his divine light. The *Exultet* proclaims, with magnificent confidence in the glorified Christ, that this is the night on which spiritual power has been given us from the risen Christ. The lighted candle we hold in our hands is the symbol of our power to live the risen life of Christ. These events take place on the level of faith, hope, and love — none of which is immediately perceptible to our senses, imagination, or emotions. But they are real, just as real as the people of Israel passing through the Red Sea; and just as real as Christ rising from the dead. It is the same saving action of God that took place in the Old Testament, was fulfilled in the New, and is now ours in this celebration of the Paschal mystery.

The sacred rites are not something we bypass in order to

reach the mystery; they are something we pass *through* to reach faith in the living Christ. Thus, the *Exultet* sings with good reason, "O holy night, O blessed night, O night that has dispelled the darkness of sin!" The liturgical darkness of this sacred night is the divine darkness that communicates to us, beyond reason and senses, the divine life that will be completely ours in eternity. The power of Christ's resurrection, symbolized by the Paschal candle and by our participation in its flame, is communicated to us inwardly, and we become the beneficiaries of his power to dispel evil, to wash away guilt, and to restore innocence. Innocence, in the scriptural sense, is intimacy with God the Father. The return to sonship is the first fruit of Christ's resurrection. As we open ourselves to the divine light, which as it grows brighter reveals the divine *life* within us, the mystery of divine life becomes the central theme of this Paschal season.

29

THE ASCENSION

*While meeting with them, he enjoined them not to depart
from Jerusalem, but to wait for "the promise of the Father
about which you have heard me speak, for John baptized
with water, but in a few days you will be baptized with the
holy Spirit."*

(Acts 1:4–5)

On Ascension Day we rejoice in the triumph of our Lord
Jesus Christ, in his exaltation to the right hand of the Father
and the glorification of his human nature. We rejoice also in
his invisible coming as a life-giving spirit into our hearts. He
goes away, but he comes again. He disappears out of this visible
world, but only to reenter it in the depths of every human heart,
there to invite us to experience the ripe fruit of his resurrection
in the overflowing power of the Holy Spirit. Today the Lord
begins to release the divine Spirit in the hearts of those who
believe, and we experience the Holy Spirit gushing forth from
our inmost being and flowing through our entire human nature.
Our thoughts, our emotions, our very bodies are aglow with the
divine Spirit. The praises of the living God pour forth upon our
lips not just from our own hearts, but from the heart of God
himself dwelling within us.

"To you," Jesus said to his disciples, "is given to know the mysteries of the reign of God." The reign of God is the high tide of light, life, and love that has been unleashed in us by the power of the resurrection and firmly established by the grace of the ascension. it is impossible to overestimate the spiritual power that is now moving within us. "Wait in Jerusalem," Jesus said, "for power from on high."

"Our God is a consuming fire," the prophet told us. Today we might say that our God is unlimited energy, a nuclear explosion that never ends. It is unlimited because its force is in God, and is God. Divine love is real power, but the very reverse of control or manipulation. It is the power to give without interruption and without end. Like the sun, it never stops radiating energy, light, and life-giving power. Even though everybody closes the curtains to hide the sun, it continues to pour itself out. The sun is a good image of God as a consuming fire. Divine love is the pouring out of light, life, and love without interruption; nor is it the least discouraged by any kind of resistance. It keeps coming.

What is our response to the grace of the Ascension? Through the readings that prepared us for this feast, Jesus proposes a new understanding of the commandment of love. He had endorsed the Old Testament teaching, which is the heart of all true morality, that we must love our neighbor as ourselves. Now he gives us a new commandment: to love one another as he has loved us, which is something infinitely more demanding. To love our neighbor as ourselves is the highest attainment of human love. But Christ is calling us not only to human love, however noble, but to divine love itself. Divine love is the capacity to love without limit and to go on loving even if all the curtains in the world are closed against us. It is to love our neighbor with unconditional acceptance. To love our neighbor as ourselves is the law of human love. It is the movement of giving and receiving — of loving and being loved in return. Hence it is concerned with the reward of love.

To love as Jesus loved us is to love with Divine Love, with the

Love of the persons of the Trinity, which is total self-surrender. They love not in order to receive love in return, but because it is the nature of divine love to give, to pour itself out, to surrender, and to do so for no other reason than because it is what it is — sheer gift. We too must love not in order to become something, but because we are called to be stewards of divine love; to be identified with it and to be channels for this immense energy, till the world is transformed by Christ and he is all in all. We surrender not because we choose to, but because Jesus has chosen us and commanded us to love as he has loved us.

When two or more persons love each other, they are united. But those who are called to divine love are called to *unity*. "Father, they are to become one as we are one." The energy of divine love has been introduced into our hearts in baptism and increased by the Eucharist and by the yearly celebration of the Resurrection. Now, on this Feast of the Ascension, we are invited to enter more deeply still into the mystery of divine life, which is the infinite exchange of divine love. The love of Christ is present in us as immense spiritual energy. The Lord Jesus asks us to exercise it and pass it on until it is our whole life. Then he will be all in all in us. He will be what he is — the glorified Christ.

30

THE ASSUMPTION

And Mary said:

> *"My soul proclaims the greatness of the Lord;*
> *my spirit rejoices in God my savior.*
> *For he has looked upon his handmaid's lowliness;*
> *behold, from now on will all ages call me blessed.*
> *The Mighty One has done great things for me,*
> *and holy is his name."*

(Luke 1:46–49)

There are three ways we might consider this feast. First, we might discuss what the feast commemorates. It commemorates the fact of our Lady's glory. This is its significance for her.

We might also consider what the significance is for us. The whole thrust of our personal history as Christians is to become what she is. We, too, are to be taken up body and soul at the resurrection.

The third point of view is the most difficult to discuss, and that is what the feast *is*. It is the most important aspect of the feast.

The Assumption of Mary is an eruption into our limited range of perception of something we desperately need to know and to experience in our inmost being. The message is that it is *safe* to be humble. It is safe to accept our lowliness and, what humanly speaking is still more disconcerting, the feeling of being nothing.

In her *Magnificat*, our Lady proclaimed, "God has looked with favor on his lowly servant in her nothingness." This was not just a pious statement. It rose up from a great depth of experience and knowledge. She knew this to be a fact. She was not afraid to acknowledge it. On the contrary, she found it to be the source of her joy: "... my spirit rejoices in God my Savior...." She was not embarrassed to be in need of a savior. She was completely at rest in the center of her nothingness.

As soon as one accepts being a creature, one enters into the creative activity of God. To accept being a creature is to be clean of the false self, to be immaculate.

Saint Thomas tells us that "the human soul is a certain capacity for God." This capacity has been joined to a material body. Perhaps we might define a human being as emptiness with a shape. The Assumption of Mary is the presence of God filling that shape. Her space became his space and his space became hers. In the degree to which we abide in our nothingness, we abide in God. And in the same degree, he can communicate himself to others through us.

This is the pattern of our Lord's human life as he explained it in John's Gospel. The eternal Word emerges from the Father without any separation. He steps forth into the world without ever leaving the Father. He works in this world, while remaining at perfect rest in the bosom of the Father. He acts, but always abides in his source.

Jesus, the Word made flesh, recommends that we too act without ever losing the awareness of our Source. "As the living Father sent me, and I live because of the Father, so he who eats me will live because of me" (John 6:57). As Jesus is united to the Father as his Source, so we are to be united to Jesus as our Source. How? Through the same means that our Lady exercised and now shares with us through the grace of her Assumption — the acceptance of our insignificance.